THE PA...
DEATH OF JESUS

THE PASSION AND
DEATH OF JESUS

HENRY WANSBROUGH OSB

DARTON·LONGMAN + TODD

First published in 2003 by
Darton, Longman and Todd Ltd
1 Spencer Court
140–142 Wandsworth High Street
London SW18 4JJ

ISBN 0 232 52510 2

A catalogue record for this book is available from the British Library.

Designed by Sandie Boccacci
Phototypeset in 10/13 Times New Roman
by Intype Libra Ltd
Printed and bound in Great Britain
by Page Bros, Norfolk.

CONTENTS

Introduction   vii

1. THE MISSION OF JESUS   1
The Quest for the Historical Jesus   1
'A Passion Narrative with Extended Introduction'   17

2. POLITICO-HISTORICAL BACKGROUND TO THE EXECUTION OF JESUS   28
The Crucifixion of Jesus a Historical Fact   28
The Governance of Judaea in the Time of Jesus   30
Pilate's Governorship of Judaea   37

3. THE AGONY IN THE GARDEN   46
Mark's Account   46
Matthew's Account   53
Luke's Account   55

4. THE ARREST   57
Mark's Account – the Betrayal   57
Matthew's Account – Jesus Betrayed   59
Luke's Account – the Captive Healer   60
John's Account – 'I Am He'   62

5. BEFORE THE HIGH PRIEST   67
Mark's Account   69
Matthew's Account   75

Luke's Account – Preparation of Charges   77
John's Account – Condemnation by Caiaphas, Confrontation
    with Annas   79

6. JESUS BEFORE PILATE   **84**
Mark's Account   84
The Interrogation before Pilate – Matthew's Account   87
The Interrogation before Pilate and Herod – Luke's Account 92
Jesus before Pilate in John   96

7. THE CRUCIFIXION   **102**
Mark's Account   102
Matthew's Account   109
Luke's Account   112
John's Account   117

ENDNOTE   **123**

Bibliography   127
Scriptural Index   130
Index of Authors and Subjects   134

INTRODUCTION

The principal aim of the writers of the gospels was to proclaim the message of Jesus, not to give an historical account of his life, of which his Passion and Death formed a central element. Each of the four evangelists sees the Passion as the climax to which the whole story of Jesus is leading, and each sees it, slightly differently, as the focus of the themes which have been important throughout the gospel. Nevertheless, the full impact of their message cannot be understood without a grasp of the historical background in first-century Palestine, occupied by the Romans. After briefly investigating the vexed question of how much we can actually know about the historical Jesus, this book aims to explain the historico-political background of the Passion of Jesus. Then each of the incidents in the Passion Narrative is examined in turn. The differences between the four accounts are investigated with a view to discovering both what actually happened (so far as is possible) and how the evangelists wish their Christian readers to understand the events. An endnote sketches the overarching theology of the saving sacrifice of the cross.

1

THE MISSION
OF JESUS

THE QUEST FOR THE HISTORICAL JESUS[1]

The basic thrust and purpose of the historical Jesus has been seen and interpreted in many ways. Did his followers later present as a religious innovator and founder of a new religious way someone who had in fact been a mistaken apocalyptic visionary, a philosopher, a social reformer, or a political revolutionary?[2] Is it possible that the gospels do not convey a true picture of Jesus? Is the true Jesus obscured rather than revealed by the gospel accounts? Did the early community fabricate a Jesus to their own liking or their own needs? Did they misunderstand or distort the true thrust of his proclamation? If they did, this must cause a major difficulty for a Christian. Surely a Christian must hold that the gospels, the inspired Word of God, constitute a reliable record? A reliable record, however, is not the same as dead-pan reporting, if such exists. A record is always interpreted. The camera, some hold, can never lie, but the selection and juxtaposition even of genuine photographs can give an interpretation of a scene. No journalist reports events without some message to convey, some impression to mediate. Even a historian writes only to convey a particular interpretation of the course of events or the career of a subject.

Every writer, before beginning to write, must decide what is important to include or exclude, and how the various elements inter-

---

[1] A succinct history of the investigation is given by Porter, 2000, pp. 1–123.
[2] A selection of the diverse viewpoints of respected modern scholars is given by Brown, 1996 at the end of his survey of the problem, pp. 824–9.

relate. Such decisions in themselves constitute personal interpretations. Every writer or narrator sees even a 'fact' from a particular point of view. A car mechanic, the driver, a policeman and an exasperated parent (owner of the car!) will report a car crash from different points of view, even if they are trying to be objective. Each holds different aspects to be important. Each will describe differently what happened; indeed, each will conceive 'what happened' differently. They will also focus on different aspects of the previous history which led up to the accident, in order better to understand what happened. Writing for colleagues, one may focus on mechanical failure, another on weather conditions, a third on impatience, a fourth on upbringing. They may interpret the event by varied literary or proverbial allusions to 'a stitch in time saves nine', 'a cloud the size of a man's hand', 'the largest parking lot in Europe', *'plus ça change, plus c'est la même chose'*.

For some decades in the mid-twentieth century it was widely held that the gospels might have some basis in history, but that they could not be considered historical works. The earliest Christians were considered simply not to have any interest in history because the imminence of the end of the world removed any point in preserving historical records, and because they failed to distinguish between the words of the historical Jesus and the words 'spoken' to the 'prophets' of the early communities in the name of the Risen Lord. The gospels were held to be unique, *sui generis* documents, conveying the message of Jesus with scant regard for any kind of history.

The first claim has been greatly moderated by recent work (see pp. 6–16). The second has been fruitfully addressed by Richard Burridge, 1992. Burridge points out that a first prerequisite for understanding any piece of writing is to know in what type of writing, what genre it falls. A love poem is to be read differently from a legal document. A report in the *Daily Telegraph*, the *Daily Mail* or the *Independent* are all to be evaluated from different points of view, according to the ends which these newspapers have. Burridge persuasively situates the gospels in the genre of biography. But within the class of biography at that time were several different sub-classes, such as laudatory biographies (*encomia*), political pamphlets under the guise of biographies, philosophical works under the guise of biographies, and biographies of properly religious figures which concentrate on the religious message. It is into the last class that the gospels fall. This means that their chief concentration is on the message and significance of the events, but without excluding the historical basis for such significance. It is, consequently, not always easy to establish exactly what did happen or exactly what was said, simply because the 'bare facts' are not the most important element. The problem must be considered in detail, and under several different headings.

THE PROBLEM

It is impossible to take the words and actions of Jesus in the gospels as literally true and exact in the way which would be provided by an unedited camcorder or tape recorder. In what sense, then, are they to be regarded as true history?

1. The words of Jesus are reported differently in different gospels. On divorce did Jesus say 'Everyone who divorces his wife, except for the case of an illicit marriage, makes her an adulteress, and anyone who marries a divorced woman commits adultery' (Matt. 5:32)? Or did he say 'Whoever divorces his wife and marries another is guilty of adultery against her. And if a woman divorces her husband and marries another she is guilty of adultery too' (Mark 10:11–12)? Or did he vary his teaching on two different occasions? How is it that the literary style of Jesus in John is indistinguishable from that of the author (where do Jesus' words end and the authorial comment begin in John 3:10–21?) and quite different from that of the synoptic Jesus?

2. Variations between different accounts of the same (or probably the same) incident show that there has been a good deal of latitude and development in the handing down of stories.[3] Are the stories of the feeding of the five thousand in Mark 6:30–44 and the feeding of the four thousand (8:1–10) in fact variant versions of the same incident? And if they are, what of Jesus' reference to them in Mark

---

[3] A personal reminiscence may help: On my first trip to the Holy Land I had considerable adventures with a Jesuit friend, Fritzleo Lentzen-Deis. When we met subsequently for the first time fifteen years later, I found that his version of our experiences had grown and veered from my sober version to the extent that I often hardly knew which incident he meant, though he usually got the punch-line right.

8:19–20 as two incidents? The story of the cure of the Canaanite woman's daughter in Matthew 15:21–28 must be the same as that of the Syro-Phoenician's daughter in Mark 7:24–30, despite differences of detail. But, to go on to a more extreme case, is the incident of the cure of the centurion of Capernaum's son (Matt. 8:5–13; Luke 7:1–10) the same as the incident of the cure of the royal official of Capernaum's son (John 4:46–53)? Furthermore, is the Matthew/Luke/John story an account of the same incident, with variations, as that narrated in the two Canaanite/Syro-Phoenician stories? Is the story of the miraculous catch of fish, followed by the call of Peter, at the beginning of Jesus' ministry (Luke 5:1–11) an account of the same incident as the account of the miraculous catch of fish, followed by the call of Peter after the resurrection (John 21:1–19)? One very obvious difference here is that the Luke story takes place early in Jesus' earthly ministry, and the John story after the resurrection.

3. Many of the incidents are crafted with a particular purpose – as is almost always the case in the telling of stories. For instance the story of the multiplication of loaves in Mark 6:30–44 is carefully crafted to bring out the parallel with 2 Kings 4:42–44 and so to show that Jesus is repeating the wonder wrought by Elisha, who in turn was repeating the wonder wrought by Moses. Thus Jesus is shown to be a new Moses. Similarly, the numbers are stylised (twelve baskets of scraps correspond to twelve tribes of Israel), and the 'green grass' in Mark 6:39 is an echo of the messianic shepherd in Psalm 23:2. By these deft touches the narrator, besides telling a story, is at the same time underlining its significance. To a casual passer-by with a camcorder, however, the scene might have seemed somewhat different.

The same interpreted re-telling of the triumphal entry into Jerusalem cannot be missed: Matthew 21:8–9 indicates that '*Very great crowds* spread their cloaks on the road, while others were cutting branches . . . and *the crowds* who went in front and those who were following . . . ' On the other hand, Mark 11:8–9 has only 'Many people . . . and those who went in front and those who followed'. Mark's account gives the basis for the flavoured and interpreted account in Matthew. Furthermore, what did the crowds cheer? Mark has them cheer 'Hosanna! *Blessed is he who comes in the name of*

the Lord. Blessed is the coming kingdom of our father David',
quoting Psalm 117, and focusing on the coming of the kingdom.
Matthew shows the crowds cheering 'Hosanna to the son of David!
Blessed is he who comes in the name of the Lord', that is, addressing
the cheers not to the kingdom but directly to Jesus himself.

4. The sequence of events is difficult or impossible to establish. The
   order of pericopes in the synoptic gospels is largely dependent on
   that given by Mark, though Matthew departs from it in clearly
   defined patterns: he presents five major sections, each composed of
   action followed by discourse, and to this end gathers together teachings (e.g. in the Sermon on the Mount, chapters 5–7) and a collection
   of ten miracles (chapters 8–9). The motives for Luke's departures
   from Mark's order may similarly be clearly catalogued. For example
   he narrates the arrest of John before the Baptism of Jesus to solve
   the embarrassing problem of Jesus submitting himself to John for
   baptism. He advances the scene of Jesus' expulsion from Nazareth
   (Mark 6:1–6) as part of his operation of creating a major prophetic
   scene by which Jesus sets out his programme in 'the Nazareth
   Manifesto' (Luke 4:16–30). On the whole, however, the order
   remains that of Mark, and Mark manifestly does not relate events
   in their chronological order, but rather groups them according to
   subject-matter. First there is a collection of healing miracles in and
   around Capernaum (1:21–2:1), then a collection of controversies
   with the Pharisees in Galilee (2:1–3:6), balanced in the second half
   of the gospel by the collection of controversies with the Jewish
   leaders in Jerusalem in 12:1–37. The positioning of the two instances
   of opening the eyes of the blind is clearly symbolic, coming as they
   do each before a major revelation, an opening of the eyes of the
   blind disciples (8:22–26; 10:46–52).

So the lynchpin of generally-accepted chronology, the week of the
Passion, may well also be a creation of Mark. This would parallel
Mark's careful spacing of Jesus' final day by mention of the hours of
prayer at third, sixth and ninth hours (15:25, 33, 34). The singing
of Psalm 118, 'Blessed is he who is coming in the name of the Lord',
and the waving of green branches (11:8–9) fit naturally into place at
the Festival of Sukkoth or Tabernacles in the autumn, rather than at the
time of the conventional Palm Sunday, just before Passover. Is it likely

that Jesus – however long or short his ministry – saved up the few days of his solitary visit to Jerusalem till the very end of his ministry, and never proclaimed his message there earlier? It has become convention to accord preference in matters of historicity to the synoptic gospels over John. But, just as John shows far more detailed and accurate knowledge of Jerusalem and of the Holy Land (Ephraim, Bethany, Bethphage, the Sheep Gate, the Pool of Bethzatha, the Pool of Siloam) than do the synoptic gospels,[4] so John's scenario of four visits to Jerusalem, often dismissed as theologically motivated, may well be more accurate.

TOWARDS SOME SOLUTIONS

For practical purposes[5] it is reasonable to begin an overview of scholarly reaction to such problems with the great work of Albert Schweitzer, *The Quest of the Historical Jesus* (1906). The original German title of this work, *Von Reimarus zu Wrede*, makes clear that the book is itself basically a survey of the earlier history of thought on the matter. Reimarus heads the procession of scholars (or speculators) surveyed by Schweitzer because in 1778, ten years after Reimarus' death, fragments of his work were published, in which he makes the important distinction between the Jesus of history (who failed to establish an earthly messianic kingdom) and the Christ of faith (to whom his followers, having stolen his body, attributed resurrection). Schweitzer surveyed the progress of the debate about the historical Jesus as far as the publication of William Wrede's *The Messianic Secret in the Gospels* in 1901. Schweitzer himself then concluded that Jesus had been a mistaken apocalyptic visionary, who went to his death in the expectation that it would introduce a new world-order. Schweitzer's famous conclusion was:

---

[4] Is John 6:17 correct in showing Jesus crossing in the boat to Capernaum, a village on the coast of the Sea of Galilee, while Mark 6:45 shows him crossing over to Bethsaida, which is now a kilometre inland from the Sea?

[5] The course of the discussion is delineated with clarity and wit in Neill and Wright, 1988. A more succinct, and therefore more schematic, account is given by Tom Wright in Wright, 1992, pp. 1–18.

> Jesus . . . in the knowledge that he is the coming Son of Man, lays hold of the wheel of the world to set it moving on that last revolution which is to bring all ordinary history to a close. It refuses to turn and he throws himself upon it. Then it does turn and crushes him. Instead of bringing in the eschatological conditions, he has destroyed them. The wheel rolls onward, and the mangled body of the one immeasurably great man, who was strong enough to think of himself as the spiritual ruler of mankind, and to bend history to his purpose, is hanging upon it still (p. 403).

The strength of Schweitzer's viewpoint was that he recognised the eschatological dimension of Jesus' message of the kingdom. Its limitation was that he understood too literally and failed to translate, or to de-code, the apocalyptic language and symbols in which this eschatological vision was expressed. Such a misunderstanding was, perhaps, more easily understandable in an age when the bulk of apocalyptic writings of the first century had only recently begun to be unearthed, and when the genre of apocalyptic was still less widely appreciated.[6] Before such nineteenth-century discoveries, this style of writing was known only from the later prophetic books of the Old Testament, especially Daniel, and from the New Testament Book of Revelation, a slim basis on which to form a rounded concept of the way apocalyptic writing works. Inherent in this genre are cosmic disturbances, lurid images of violence, figures moving easily between earth and heaven (in both directions), heraldic and speaking animals and far-reaching symbolism derived from the Old Testament. The basic message of such literature is always reassurance that God will soon intervene to rescue his people from persecution. But prediction of concrete events plays little or no part in the prophetic writings, which seek to interpret history rather than to foretell how it will unfold. Against this background the apocalyptic sayings of the gospels take on a very different feel, and so a very different meaning, and can hardly form a basis for the view that Jesus expected this space-time continuum to cease to exist with his death.

The scholarly world scarce had time to digest Schweitzer's findings

---

[6] A preliminary publication of the Ethiopic text of the Book of Enoch was made in 1838, but the first critical edition appeared only in 1906. The first translation of the Syriac Apocalypse of Baruch into a modern language was published in 1896.

before the outbreak of the First World War. Immediately after the First World War concentration switched to the new methods of Form Criticism, one of whose presuppositions was that it is impossible to penetrate to the bedrock of what actually happened in the lifetime of Jesus. A basic position of the Form Critics was that we can go no further back in history than to trace the influences, questions and concerns of the early communities which shaped the units of the gospel tradition. The first generation of Christians was so concerned with the imminent coming of the Day of the Lord that they had no time for history. They had no interest in conserving the memory of their founder. That colossus, Rudolf Bultmann, whose influence dominated New Testament scholarship during the middle decades of the twentieth century, particularly held that research into the life of Jesus was an impossibility. Adopting the position of William Wrede (*The Messianic Secret in the Gospels*, 1901, but translated into English only in 1971), Bultmann held, for instance, that Jesus never thought of himself as Messiah, or claimed to be Messiah. It was his disciples, after his death, who invented these claims, and worked them into the accounts of his ministry. The inventive power of the Christian community was immense. According to Bultmann, the story of the testing of Jesus in the desert, more elaborate in Matthew and Luke than in Mark, was pure invention: 'The story of the temptation is a legend which arose out of reflection on the quality of Jesus as Messiah, or rather on the nature of the Christian belief in Jesus as Messiah'.[7] Indeed, on theological grounds Bultmann declared that it was not even desirable to return to the 'Christ according to the flesh', for 'It is not the Christ according to the flesh who is the Lord, but Jesus Christ as he is encountered in the proclamation.'[8]

Such was Bultmann's authority that reputable scholars[9] no longer attempted the task which Bultmann had declared to be impossible and mistaken, of establishing the true facts of Jesus' life. It was not until 1953 that one of Bultmann's former students, by now himself a prestigious professor, Ernst Käsemann, in a lecture entitled 'The Problem of the Historical Jesus', reversed this trend and initiated what

---

[7] Bultmann, 1974, p. 27.

[8] Bultmann, 1961, p. 208.

[9] With rare exceptions, such as C. H. Dodd in England and Joachim Jeremias in Germany, seen in their writings on the parables of Jesus.

has become known as 'The New Quest of the Historical Jesus'. The New Quest was concerned principally with the authenticity of the sayings of Jesus, rather than his deeds. It set out to establish criteria by which these sayings may be judged authentic or inauthentic. It operated, of course, against the background of the accepted and permanent findings of the Form Critics that the needs, concerns and problems of the earliest communities played an important part in the handing down of the tradition and in the formation of the gospels.[10]

A variety of criteria for separating out the authentic words of Jesus was proposed, such as:

- **Multiple Attestation.** A saying is historically reliable if it is attested in several different sources, not simply in Mark (and derivatively in Matthew and Luke), and the hypothetical Sayings Source 'Q', but also in John, whose material is deemed to represent an independent tradition.[11] It is more reliable still if the tradition is contained also in Paul. An instance of this would be the narrative of the institution of the eucharist, given in both the synoptic gospels and 1 Corinthians 11. Another is Jesus' objection to the Jewish tolerance of divorce, present in both the synoptic gospels and 1 Corinthians 7. The major difficulty about this criterion is that even in the score of years between Jesus' ministry and 1 Corinthians, a tradition foisted on Jesus a dozen years after his death could have taken the slightly divergent forms attested in the gospels and 1 Corinthians.
- **Friend and Foe.** If Jesus' friends and foes concur in asserting something it has a high claim to historicity. An instance of this would be Jesus' exorcisms, since the opponents of Jesus, in explaining away Jesus' exorcisms by his alliance with Satan or Beelzebul (Mark 3:21–26), tacitly admitted that such exorcisms occurred.
- **Criterion of Embarrassment.** The progressive silence of the gospels on the humiliations of Jesus' Passion and Death confirm what is obvious, that it was embarrassing for Christians to admit that their leader died the humiliating and disgusting death of a criminal slave.

---

[10] An important statement of the Pontifical Biblical Commission on historicity of the gospels, already in 1964, distinguishes three stages of development, that of Jesus, that of the apostolic community and that of the writers of the gospels.

[11] This criterion was already developed as long ago as 1906 in Burkitt, 1906, pp. 147–68.

The crucifixion would hardly have been invented by the followers of Jesus if it had not happened. Similarly the gospels show a degree of embarrassment at the Baptism of Jesus: how is it that Jesus submitted himself to John's baptism, thereby joining a community of repentant sinners and tacitly classing himself as a repentant sinner? Mark describes the incident with John the Baptist. Then Matthew shows his embarrassment by inserting (inventing?) a snippet of dialogue, in which Jesus explains to the Baptist that the baptism is not John's action on Jesus, but their joint action 'it is fitting *for us* so to fulfil all justice' (Matt. 3:14–15). Luke takes a more radical solution, by first describing the arrest of John, and then not mentioning John at all in the baptism scene. In addition, by Luke the focus is taken off the baptism itself, which becomes only a time-marker for the descent of the Spirit on Jesus to begin his ministry (as the descent of the Spirit on the disciples at Pentecost begins their ministry).

- **Criterion of Dissimilarity.** This criterion, to which Norman Perrin (one of the earliest pioneers of this technique) ascribes the greatest importance, is also the strictest. A saying is regarded as authentic if its content is at variance both with the Judaism which preceded Jesus and with the doctrines and interests of the young Christian community. It cannot, therefore, stem either from another contemporary teacher or from the early community. This criterion has three unsatisfactory features. Firstly, it is too strict, and must exclude many of Jesus' authentic sayings. Secondly, we do not know enough about the highly varied contemporary Judaism to be sure that a saying is in disharmony with all the currents of contemporary Judaism. Thirdly, it leaves Jesus without forebears from the past and without influence for the future. One saying which passes this test is the shocking saying, 'Leave the dead to bury their dead' (Matt. 8:22).

The difficulty of this process, however, was the application of these criteria. Scholars differed widely about whether such and such a saying was shown by these criteria to be authentic. Perhaps the ultimate absurdity of the use of the method was reached in The Jesus Seminar, a fraternity of scholars who began in 1985 to meet twice a year in various North American universities to study the sayings of Jesus, colour-coding them for authenticity from red ('That's Jesus') through pink and grey to black ('There's been some mistake').[12] An extreme product of the strong anti-historical attitude of this Seminar may be found in Gerd Lüdemann's book, *Jesus after 2000 Years, What He Really Said and Did* (SCM Press, 2000). Lüdemann discusses in turn every unit of the gospels, considering successively redaction, tradition and historical yields. Judgements abound in this vein: on Mark 7:24–30, 'The historical yield is nil, as the narrative must be derived from debates in the early Christian community' (p. 51). On John 6:35, 'This saying is inauthentic. Jesus did not understand himself as a bringer of salvation' (p. 471). Lüdemann's lame conclusion is, 'I have come to the conclusion that Jesus is a sympathetic, original figure, a man of wit and humour at whom I sometimes chuckle. But . . . he sometimes becomes too serious for me. In his confident dialogue with God, Jesus seems to me almost ridiculous, for here he makes the mistake of so many religious people: he sees himself at the centre of the world' (p. 692).

A new and different approach was pioneered by E. P. Sanders, which has been characterised by N. T. Wright as 'The Third Quest'.[13] For Sanders the starting-point is not the sayings, each considered in isolation, but the actions of Jesus, and more specifically the action of Jesus in the Temple, which he regards as the key to Jesus' whole attitude and ministry. With brilliant, painstaking and original research Sanders set about replacing Jesus in his Jewish context, and specifically in the context of an eschatological mission. Jesus' eschatology was a restoration eschatology, in that he set out not to destroy but to restore Judaism. At the time of Jesus the Jews still felt they had never really overcome the Babylonian Exile: it still persisted in the shape of the Roman enslavement of their country. Jesus' purpose was to bring about in a new way the long-expected and final reign of God. The climax of his work was the demonstration in the Temple that the old and still current ways of Judaism were sterile and must be swept away. Sanders investigated the contemporary background to Jesus' mission in a series of careful studies, such as *Jesus and Judaism* (SCM Press, 1985),

---

[12] The methods and process of The Jesus Seminar are described and excoriated by Luke Timothy Johnson in Johnson, 1996, pp. 1–27.

[13] Porter is not alone in insisting (Porter, 2000, p. 52–5) that recent research and methods are not sufficiently distinct to merit classification of a third quest, distinguished from the New Quest.

Judaism, Practice and Belief, 63 BCE – 66 CE (SCM Press, 1992), and the resulting picture is filled out in *The Historical Figure of Jesus* (Allen Lane, 1993).

Nevertheless, Sanders also gives a fairly narrow inventory of basic facts about Jesus which are 'almost beyond dispute':

1. Jesus was born c. 4 BC near the time of the death of Herod the Great.
2. He spent his childhood and early adult years in Nazareth, a Galilean village.
3. He was baptised by John the Baptist.
4. He called disciples.
5. He taught in the towns, villages and countryside of Galilee (apparently not the cities).
6. He preached 'the kingdom of God'.
7. About the year AD 30 he went to Jerusalem for Passover.
8. He created a disturbance in the Temple area.
9. He had a final meal with the disciples.
10. He was arrested and interrogated by the Jewish authorities, specifically the High Priest.
11. He was executed on the orders of the Roman prefect, Pontius Pilate.[14]

At the same time, the extent to which Sanders diverges from the picture of Jesus acceptable to popular piety – and the conjectural nature of a reconstruction – may be seen from his outline of the death of Jesus:

> It is possible that, when Jesus drank his last cup of wine and predicted that he would drink it again in the kingdom, he thought that the kingdom would arrive immediately. After he had been on the cross for a few hours, he despaired, and cried out that he had been forsaken. This speculation is only one possible explanation. We do not know what he thought as he hung in agony on the cross. After a relatively short period of suffering he died, and some of his followers and sympathisers hastily buried him.[15]

Sanders' basic picture of Jesus' endeavour has been highly influential.

---

14 Sanders, 1993, pp. 10–11.
15 Sanders, 1993, pp. 274–5.

There have not, however, been lacking other reconstructions of his fundamental orientation. One of the earliest pictures in the New Quest was that of S. G. F. Brandon. In *Jesus and the Zealots* (1967) he argued from the fact that Jesus was crucified by the Romans that he was a violent revolutionary, after the pattern of the Zealots who spearheaded the Jewish Revolt in AD 66. Jesus' disciples then falsely presented him as a religious rather than a political leader – insofar as the two can, in a theocratic situation like Judaism, be distinguished. One persuasive point in Brandon's argument was that a large proportion of the disciples have nationalistic names, names held by the heroic Maccabean resistance leaders two centuries before, such as Judas, John and Simon; did Jesus deliberately choose his inner core of followers from among nationalists? In general, however, Brandon's interpretation is not convincing. Possibly the strongest point against it is that there is no evidence in Jesus' day for violent or Zealot activity. There was indeed some unrest in the years immediately after the death of Herod the Great in 4 BC, but little during Jesus' adulthood and ministry. He would have been an isolated figure of political protest. The real unrest which escalated into the Jewish Revolt began only in AD 44.

Another attempt at interpreting Jesus was pioneered in 1988 by F. Gerald Downing.[16] Downing's starting-point is that the Galilee of Jesus' time was highly hellenised, and Greek would have been currently spoken. Further, 'our early Christian documents are addressed to people for whom it was natural to converse and think in Greek' (p. v). Downing observes that Jesus' disciples were sent out more or less in the same guise as Cynic preachers. The Cynics were popular philosophers who radically questioned the whole basis of the accepted criteria of success in that and any age, namely wealth and prestige. Their wandering teachers dressed in much the same way as the Christian missionaries are instructed to do in Matthew 9:35–10:16; Mark 6:7–11, etc. 'A raggedly cloaked and outspoken figure with no luggage and no money would not just have looked Cynic, he would obviously have wanted to' (p. vi). Downing then assembles a collection of Cynic sayings and teachings which are not entirely dissimilar to some of those of Jesus in the gospels. For instance parallels to 'It is not the healthy who need

---

[16] Downing, 1998.

the doctor but the sick. I came to call not the upright but sinners'
(Mark 2:17) are given as Antisthenes' remark, 'Physicians can attend
the sick without catching the fever' and Diogenes' saying, 'The sun
visits dung-heaps without getting dirty' (p. 122). Jesus' sayings on
forgiveness are put in parallel to Seneca's question, 'Who gets angry
with a patient he is trying to cure?' (p. 123). Such a position encounters
a host of difficulties:

- It is highly doubtful whether Galilee in the early first century was so
  strongly hellenised or that Greek was currently and widely spoken.
  Evidence of hellenisation and spoken Greek drawn from centuries,
  or even decades, later (e.g. a series of tombs dated from the first to
  the third century[17]) is irrelevant. The early Christian writings were
  not written down for the inhabitants of Galilee, and the gospels in
  many cases show strong traces of an underlying Aramaic speech
  in the sayings of Jesus.
- The sayings catalogued as parallel to those of the gospels are only
  distantly similar to gospel teachings, though the gospel sayings do
  share with them the outspoken criticism of current systems of value,
  and especially the emphasis on human dignity and respect for indi-
  viduals.
- There is no parallel in these Cynic sayings of Jesus' overwhelming
  sense of his mission from God to establish the reign of God. There
  is no echo of the eschatological ring which sounds so strongly in all
  Jesus' teaching. The miracles, which formed such an important part
  of the tradition of Jesus and his followers, are totally lacking.

A slightly different background is presupposed by John Dominic
Crossan.[18] He holds that Jesus does indeed fit well against the background of the Cynics, in a world of aristocratic and plutocratic
oppression. He characterises Jesus and his followers as 'hippies in a
world of Augustan yuppies' (p. 421). There is, however, a difference:
the Cynics exercised their mission in the cities, whereas Jesus and his
followers were peasant Jewish Cynics: 'his work was among the farms
and villages of Lower Galilee' (p. 422), in a countryside crippled by

---

[17] See discussion of how widespread Greek-speaking was in Galilee in the first
    century in Porter 2000, pp. 171–6.
[18] In Crossan, 1991.

heavy and multiple taxation and mulcted by absentee landlords. Nazareth is so insignificant a village that the first mention of it outside
Christian sources is a third- or fourth-century inscription found at
Caesarea. After the Baptist's arrest Jesus diverged from John's eschatological message and set about proclaiming direct access to God, 'the
brokerless kingdom of God', bypassing all the conventional means of
success, even religious success, by 'a religious and economic egali-
tarianism that negated alike and at once the hierarchical and patronal
normalcies of Jewish religion and Roman power' (p. 422). In fact,
however, the evidence for crushing taxation and for large numbers of
absentee landlords in Galilee is as imaginary as the evidence for widespread hellenisation.[19] There is no reason to suppose that Hellenistic
culture had outstripped Jewish. There is no reason to deny that synagogues were widespread, and the recent excavations at Sepphoris, the
administrative capital of Lower Galilee, show that there was a rigorous
and observant Jewish life there in the mid first century.

Quite different is the position of Geza Vermes, who, at least since
the publication of his *Jesus the Jew* in 1973, has been writing to
depict Jesus against a thoroughly Jewish background in Galilee, which
Josephus repeatedly presents as agriculturally prosperous, a sort of
fertile Garden of Eden (*Jewish War* 2.592; 3.42–43; 516–519). Vermes
plays down any notion of a heavy hellenised or bilingual Galilee, and
'as for Jesus being a Greek speaker, this is a wild flight of fancy'
(Vermes, 2000, p. 227). He depicts Jesus among the charismatic Galilean rabbis, about whom so many touching stories abound in the ancient
Jewish Mishnah. One such was Rabbi Honi the Rain-Maker, so called
because he persuaded God to send rain to end a three-year drought.
About him and to him a contemporary, a leading Pharisee, wrote, 'You
pester God, yet he performs your will, like a son who pesters his father
and obtains from him what he wants' (p. 247). Typical of the miracle
stories of these charismatic Galilean rabbis is one about Rabbi Hanina
ben Dosa:

> It happened that there was a snake in the locality which injured
> people. They went and reported it to R. Hanina ben Dosa. He said
> to them, 'Show me its hole.' He placed his heel on the entrance

---

[19] E. P. Sanders in Donnelly, 2001, pp. 9–22.

of the hole, and the snake come out, bit him and died. He put it on his shoulder [so disregarding purity-regulations] and carried it to the school. He said to them, 'See, my children, it is not the snake that kills, but sin.' In that hour they framed the saying, 'Woe to the man who meets a snake, but woe to the snake that meets R. Hanina ben Dosa' (p. 244).

The miracle, the disregard for the interpretation of the purity Law, the pithy, balanced saying, all are reminiscent of the stories about Jesus in the synoptic gospels. Yet Vermes grants that Jesus towers over all these contemporary figures, 'Jesus was a solitary giant among the ancient Hasidim' (p. 256), by the perceptiveness of his teaching, the strength of his resolve and, above all, by his eschatological outlook in declaring the nearness and the actual presence of the kingdom of God.

Enough examples have been given to show what diverse evaluations have been made of the historicity of the sayings and deeds of Jesus given in the gospels, and how widely differing are the interpretations by even respected mainline scholars. The gospels cannot be treated as naïve or straightforward history, written according to the canons of modern history or modern factual reportage. Or can they? This question must be addressed not only to the gospels but also to 'the canons of modern history or modern factual reportage'. The difference between the technique of the modern historian and the technique of the evangelist is that the modern historian claims to separate the account of the event from the interpretation, while the evangelist weaves into the account the interpretation which he and the community perceive in the event. Just as a modern account may bring out the meaning and significance of an event by allusion or comparison to a previous well-known event which the historian considers a parallel,[20] so the evangelist frequently inclines to bring out the sacred significance of an event in the life of Jesus by allusion and comparison to passages in the sacred books, the Bible.

What, then, are the gospels, and has the story told in them been stretched and packaged to point a lesson? Our subject is the Passion

---

[20] A film could poignantly and effectively use Tchaikowsky's *1812 Overture* as background music to Hitler's disastrous invasion of Russia during the Second World War, to underline that it was a repeat of Napoleon's disaster in 1812.

and Death of Jesus, so that our primary question is whether the whole story is told with an eye to or affected by these final events of the story of Jesus. It is arguable that the evangelists see the Passion and Death as the climax of Jesus' whole life, and so present it as leading inevitably to these events, to the extent that they can already be sensed in the earlier events of his life.

'A PASSION NARRATIVE WITH EXTENDED INTRODUCTION'

As long ago as 1892 Martin Kähler described the gospel of Mark as 'a passion narrative with extended introduction'. The same may be said of all the gospels. The Passion comes as no surprise, but has been prepared for throughout the gospel; it is the summit without which the gospel would make no sense. In each of the gospels the expectation of the Passion has been woven into all the preceding narrative. The reader senses and knows right from the beginning that Jesus is the Christ who is destined to suffer and to die.

MARK

In the first gospel, Mark, expectation of the Passion permeates the gospel particularly on three levels.

Firstly, the reader is prepared for the Passion by the frequent allusions or 'flash-forwards' which occur. The clue to the gospel is given in the Voice from heaven at the baptism. This is the climax of Mark's brief introduction which shows the reader who Jesus is, before the reader settles back to watch the disciples themselves discovering slowly, so slowly, who Jesus is. The introduction provides the basis for the characteristic Markan feature of irony, a narration on two levels, when the reader understands what is happening at a different level from the understanding of the actors on the ground. At the same time the actors are discovering that Jesus is first the Messiah and then the suffering Messiah, while the reader, already knowing that Jesus is, in some sense, 'son of God', is discovering fully by the action which unrolls in the course of the gospel what it means to be 'son of God'. But already in the Voice from heaven there is a hint of the Passion. The words of the Voice, 'You are my son, the beloved; in you I am well pleased' form an allusion to the opening of the Servant Songs in Isaiah 42:1. The Servant of the Lord in Isaiah is to suffer and be humiliated, achieving vindication and the glory of God only through suffering. If Jesus is being called to be the Servant, then the 'favour' of God includes suffering and rejection. Such is the destiny already appointed to Jesus at his baptism.

Next, in the controversies with the Pharisees in 2:1–3:6, a similar hint occurs at crucial points. The controversies are skilfully arranged in a chiasmus,[21] highlighting the Passion at the two key spots, the centre and the end. In the centre comes the hint, 'The time will come when the bridegroom is taken away from them' (2:20).[22] Similarly at the end the outcome of the controversies is a warning of persecution to come: 'The Pharisees went out and began at once to plot with the Herodians against him, how they might destroy him' (3:6). The rest of the chapter is devoted to the deepening opposition to Jesus, even from his own family, presented in a typically Markan 'sandwich': family – scribes – family (3:13–35).[23] This represents a crescendo of opposition, to which Jesus finally reacts with the parable of the sower, a summative comment on his inability to attract a widespread and loyal following: most of the seed goes to waste, and only a small proportion of it produces an increasingly encouraging yield, thirtyfold, sixtyfold, or a

---

[21] The first member balances the last, the second balances the penultimate, the third balances the propenultimate, focusing the accent on the central core:
    a. Cure of a Paralytic – controversy within a healing-story
    b. Food controversy, ending with a proverb
    c. Double-saying about fasting
    *The Bridegroom taken away
    c. Double-saying about novelty
    b. Food controversy, ending with proverb
    a. Cure of the Withered Hand – controversy within a healing-story.

[22] This must surely be an allegorisation due to Mark. It would hardly be intelligible to the bystanders at the time, certainly so early in Jesus' ministry, before they have had any hint of violence. Some sort of explanation in the parable is required for the extraordinary happening of the bridegroom being 'taken away', hardly an everyday occurrence. The style with its oral duality 'then, on that day' is typically Markan (see Neirynck, 1988).

[23] Mark frequently 'intercalates' or 'sandwiches' an incident between two others in such a way that the extremes and the centre illustrate each other, e.g. healing/forgiveness/healing (2:1–12), where the visible power of Jesus to heal illustrates his invisible power to forgive; fig-tree/temple-cleansing/fig-tree (11:13–20), where the barrenness of the fig-tree is a symbol of the barrenness of the temple-cult.

hundredfold. Very soon, the fate of the Baptist at the hands of Herod will itself be warning enough for those who have heard the similarity of Jesus' preaching to that of John. It is further stressed by the ominous, 'they came and took his corpse and laid it in a tomb' (6:29), the same phrase, with the same rough word for 'corpse/body'[24] as occurs of Jesus' burial in 15:45–46.

A second indication of the inevitability of the Passion is provided by the consistent emphasis on the certainty of persecution for the disciples. Mark frequently indicates emphasis by triple repetition, and nowhere in a more pronounced fashion than in the events of the Passion.[25] So the Passion is formally prophesied by Jesus three times. Each of these great formal prophecies of the Passion (8:31; 9:31; 10:32–34) is followed by a misunderstanding by the disciples and a reiteration by Jesus that sharing his sufferings is a prerequisite for being a disciple: 'If anyone wants to be a follower of mine, let him renounce himself and take up his cross and follow me' (8:34); 'if anyone wants to be first, he must make himself last of all and servant of all' (9:35). Finally, to the sons of Zebedee who ask for seats at his right and left Jesus can promise only, 'The cup that I shall drink, you shall drink' (10:39). The company with Jesus, on his right and left, will be the company kept by the two criminals crucified with him, a grim Markan irony! Most strongly of all, the accent of Mark 13, the long discourse on the future of the followers of Jesus – by far the longest and most carefully-crafted single discourse in Mark – is all on the inevitability of persecution to be undergone by his disciples, from which they will eventually be delivered: 'You will be handed over to sanhedrins; you will be beaten in synagogues, and you will be brought before governors and kings for my sake' (Mark 13:9).

Thirdly, and perhaps most significantly of all, the disciples cannot understand their Master until they have seen and realised in experience that Jesus can reach his destiny only through the Passion. Immediately after the Transfiguration they are warned that they should 'tell no one what they had seen until after the Son of man had risen from the dead' (Mark 9:9). It is at the moment of Jesus' death that the climax occurs.

---

[24] Πτῶμα rather than the gentler σῶμα.
[25] Three accusations before the High Priest, Peter's three denials, Pilate's three assertions of Jesus' innocence, the threefold division of the day.

The first human being to acknowledge Jesus as 'son of God[26] is the centurion at the foot of the cross. This is a clear signal that Jesus' true quality of divine sonship is revealed only in his suffering and death. No wonder the disciples were forbidden to proclaim the message when they had been able to understand only a preliminary part of it, still needing to be completed by an understanding of the centrality of the Passion to a full comprehension of Jesus' person and significance.

MATTHEW

Each of the evangelists has his own way of bringing the coming Passion to the attention of his audience. Matthew hints at it already in the infancy story by Herod's attempt to kill the child after the Magi slip away (Matt. 2:16–18). The murderous Jewish king contrasts with the appreciative gentile Wise Men, presaging the future hostile reaction of his subjects – just as at the end condemnatory Jewish crowds ('His blood be on us and on our children') contrast with the acquitting gentile Pilate ('I find no cause in him').

The presage of suffering for the community is further ominously stressed in the Beatitudes. The eight Beatitudes themselves form a finely wrought and beautifully balanced poem,[27] coming to a climax in the final Beatitude, 'Blessed are those who are persecuted in the cause of righteousness; the Kingdom of Heaven is theirs' (5:10). Not only is this the final Beatitude placed in a key position, but it is also stressed by immediate repetition in the more direct and forceful second person, 'Blessed are you when people abuse you and persecute you and speak all kinds of calumny against you falsely on my account' (5:11). Nor is this the only hint of future persecution in the Sermon on the Mount. The central third petition of the Lord's Prayer, 'Thy will be done on

---

[26] Should this be written 'Son of God' or 'son of God'? There are no special capital letters in Greek, or rather all the letters in the early manuscripts are capitals, so that it is impossible to make the distinction. Capitalisation therefore depends on the level of discourse. The centurion's acknowledgement is a typical piece of Markan irony. The Roman centurion surely meant his statement in terms of his own, presumably polytheistic, religious experience and language. But he is saying more than he realises, and the Christian reader understands his words on a quite different level.

[27] See Puéch, 1991, pp. 80–106, and Green, 2001.

earth as in heaven' (6:10), inevitably acquires the overtones of the
Passion through its repetition by Jesus during the agony in the garden
(see p. 54). When he comes to teach about the daily life of the community, in his second great discourse, the discourse on mission in
chapter 10 (10:16–31), Matthew also strengthens the stress on the
persecution of the disciples by making it the hallmark of the destiny
of the missioners of the gospel. Nevertheless, he does not lessen this
message in the chapter corresponding to Mark 13 (Matt. 24).

It is neither certain nor relevant exactly where or when Matthew was
writing, but tension between Matthew's community and other Jews,
personalised in 'the scribes and Pharisees', runs through the book.
Matthew's values are those of Judaism. From the beginning he presents
Jesus as son of David[28] and second Moses.[29] The moral values which
he presents are those of fulfilment of the Law, but in the new way of
Jesus. In the Sermon on the Mount, Jesus shows how his followers'
justice (δικαιοσύνη) must exceed the justice of the scribes and Pharisees, fulfilling scripture more perfectly than scribes and Pharisees can
ever claim to do. At the same time, Matthew hints that – in contrast to
Mark's community – in his community those 'boundary-markers' of
Judaism, sabbath and food-laws, were still observed.[30] This strong
emphasis on Judaism makes the criticism of the scribes and Pharisees
(23:1–36) all the more confrontational. The disciples are warned that
'they will hand you over to sanhedrins and in their synagogues you
will be flogged' (10:17) and that hostility will bring division right
inside families (10:34–35).

Whether a formal break has occurred between Matthew's kind of
Judaism and a more normative Jewish community has been hotly disputed, but certainly they were on the cusp of such a break, and felt

---

[28] Beginning with the proud drum-roll of the great ancestors of Judaism, chapter 1
reaches its climax with the adoption of Jesus by divine command into the house
of David when Joseph names the child – a way of accepting the child as his own
son.

[29] King Herod's unsuccessful attempt to eliminate the child parallels Pharaoh's
attempt to eliminate Moses. The flight of the holy family into a foreign land and
their return at a divine message parallel the flight of Moses and his family into
Midian, and their return at an angelic message.

[30] His community are to pray (24:20) that their flight on the Day of the Lord is not
hampered by Sabbath restrictions. He also deliberately omits (15:17) Mark's
liberating 'thus he made all foods clean' (Mark 7:19).

themselves to be a persecuted minority. An unprovable but imagina-tively helpful context for such a community of Jewish disciples of Jesus as the Christ is the large Jewish community at Antioch on the Syrian coast, where his followers were first called 'Christians' (Acts 11:26). Here after the Sack of Jerusalem in AD 70 the Jews themselves were persecuted by their gentile townsfolk. The role of persecuted minority of a persecuted minority would have sharpened hostility to the degree which underlies much of Matthew's writing, and accounts for the tension which is so palpable in his gospel.

LUKE

In his own way Luke also makes the Passion the backbone at least of the second half of the gospel, in the form of the great journey up to Jerusalem (Luke 9:51–18:14), where Jesus the prophet is to perish, since 'it would not be right for a prophet to die away from Jerusalem' (13:33). But already earlier there have been sinister developments.

Even before Jesus' ministry begins we are ominously warned by Simeon's dire prediction to Mary that the child is destined to be a sign which will be opposed, and that a sword will pierce her own heart (Luke 2:35). Again, at the end of the story of the testing in the desert, the devil leaves Jesus, but only 'until the opportune moment' (4:13), leaving the reader in suspense as to when this opportune moment will arrive. This opportune moment begins when 'Satan entered into Judas', leading him to make his pact with the chief priests (22:3).

When the ministry begins Luke treats us to one of those masterly scenes in which he conveys a rich theological lesson in the form of an historical story. He transforms the scene of the expulsion from Nazareth, making it into a microcosm of the whole process of Jesus' ministry.[31] Taking the clue from Jesus' saying in Mark, 'A prophet is only without honour in his own homeland', Luke makes it (Luke 4:16–30) the occasion for a sort of prophetic manifesto, in which Jesus, filled with the Spirit, likens himself to the prophets Elijah and Elisha in bringing salvation to those outside Israel, stressing at the same time that this is the fulfilment of Isaiah's prophecy. To complete the microcosmic scene,

---

[31] Just as the Journey to Emmaus is a microcosm of the process of the apostolate.

instead of merely not being able to work any miracles there, Jesus survives an assassination attempt, of which there was no sign in Mark, as he 'passed straight through the crowd and walked away'.

The great journey up to Jerusalem becomes ever more ominous. The signal for it is given at the Transfiguration, where the three figures are discussing the ἔξοδος/'exit' (9:31) which Jesus 'is destined to accomplish at Jerusalem'. The actual start to the journey could hardly be more dramatic: literally, 'And it happened [a solemn biblical formula] at the fulfilment of the days of his being taken up [the same word as is used of the Ascension], he tensed his face to set off for Jerusalem' (9:51). Then the principal content and teaching to the disciples on the journey is on the hardships of the apostolic calling, which again and again include the threat of rejection and persecution after the model of their Master, building up the tension and expectation of what is to happen at Jerusalem with such sayings as 'I have come to bring fire to the earth, and how I wish it were blazing already! There is a baptism which I must receive, and what constraint I am under until it is completed!' (12:49–50). At roughly the mid-point of the journey Jesus already laments over Jerusalem, affectionately repeating the name, 'Jerusalem, Jerusalem, you that kill the prophets and stone those who are sent to you. How often have I longed to gather your children together, as a hen gathers her brood under her wings, and you refused!' (13:34). The intensity of Jesus' efforts to convert Jerusalem, and so the daring of his confrontation with the authorities, is heightened by his teaching every day in the Temple (the bracket which encloses, and so interprets, his Jerusalem ministry, 19:47 and 21:37), and by the explicit frustration of the authorities, who 'could not find a way to do anything because the whole people hung on his words' (19:48). The forward movement continues to build right through to the Last Supper, when Jesus almost expresses his impatience to reach his goal, 'I have ardently longed to eat this Passover with you before I suffer, because I tell you, I shall not eat it until it is fulfilled in the kingdom of God' (22:15–16). But by now the inevitable conclusion has been locked into place by Satan entering into Judas.

JOHN

John's style of teaching is overwhelmingly allusive and ironical. By
these means the reader is kept constantly aware of the impending
Passion, Death and Resurrection. This gospel is full of hints and deeper
layers of meaning which can be seen and appreciated by those who
will see them, by those who already have some understanding of the
message, though on the surface such hints lack significance or seem
merely poetical. Typical of this allusiveness are the three terms 'the
hour', 'lifted up' and 'glorified'.

From the beginning of the gospel Jesus is awaiting a mysterious
'hour', and by his expectation heightens the tension also for the reader.
So at the marriage-feast at Cana he first tells his mother that he cannot
solve the embarrassment of the young couple because his hour has not
yet come (2:4), though he later mysteriously retracts this refusal. What
is this 'hour'? We do not know, but it must be some moment of
consummation or of reaching a goal, some moment aimed at in some
particular way. This is a supreme example of Johannine irony, when
the reader in fact knows, but by the demands of the story is invited
dramatically to suspend this knowledge, just as we are invited to
suspend knowledge when the soldiers mock Jesus as king (19:3) or the
chief priests encourage Pilate to write only that Jesus *claimed to be*
King of the Jews (19:21). We know full well – what the actors in the
drama do not know – that he really is king.

Repeatedly the mention of the hour awakens the reader's expectation
and accelerates the forward movement of the gospel. Mysterious, almost
furtive, reminders of this significant moment do little to relieve the
puzzlement. 'The hour is coming when you will worship the Father
neither on this mountain nor in Jerusalem ... The hour is coming –
indeed is already here – when true worshippers will worship the Father
in spirit and in truth' (4:21, 23), says Jesus to the Samaritan. It is an
hour which from one point of view is still in the future, from another
already present, a decisive moment when true worship will come to
fulfilment, freed from the constraints of locality. Not long afterwards,
the same formula reappears in the account of the controversy in Jerusalem, an hour present yet future, 'The hour is coming – indeed it is
already here – when the dead will hear the voice of the Son of God
and all who hear it will live' (5:25). From the point of view of the

actors, the hour is still to come; from the point of view of writer and audience, it is already present and effective. Paradoxically and ungrammatically, both angles are expressed simultaneously. In the life of Jesus it is a goal in the future; in the life of the Church it is a present reality, determining the conditions and expectations of life. A more threatening expectation, and mounting tension, is expressed in other clashes in Jerusalem, when no one laid a hand on him 'because his hour had not yet come' (7:30; 8:20).

The tension finally begins to mount sharply in the last scene of the ministry, when the leaders of the Jews have already decided to do away with Jesus, since 'it is better that one man should die for the people than that the whole nation should perish', as the High Priest says with consummate Johannine irony (11:50). The Johannine equivalent of the agony in the garden brings a bright focus on the hour. Jesus is filled with anguish at the approach of the hour, and yet he cannot – as he does in the synoptic gospels – pray that it should pass him by: 'Now my soul is troubled. What shall I say? "Father, save me from this hour"? But it is for this very reason that I have come to this hour' (12:27). Jesus is utterly focused on this hour, and we begin to see the dual aspect of the hour of which we have heard so much. It is an hour of dread as well as an hour of accomplishment, since Jesus continues immediately, 'Father, glorify your name' (12:28). As a banner-headline over the whole Passion Story stands the solemn declaration of Jesus' acceptance of all that is to come, 'Jesus, knowing that his hour had come to pass from this world to the Father' (13:1), repeated at the opening of the High Priestly prayer (17:1), 'Father, the hour has come'. Thus throughout the story of Jesus the hour is woven into the fabric of the narrative as a destined and unalterable factor of the future.

The second vehicle of allusive expectation is the expression 'lifted up'. As with so many Johannine expressions, it is fertile with misunderstanding. Nicodemus misunderstands birth (ἄνωθεν) as being a second physical birth when Jesus means birth 'from above' (3:3–6). The Samaritan misunderstands the ambiguous offer of 'living water', taking it to be fresh water when Jesus really means the water of life. The Jews misunderstand Jesus' teaching about eating his flesh as cannibalism (6:52). It is as though misunderstanding is a deliberate policy of Jesus' teaching, to provoke the puzzled question which in John so often leads on to further explanation. So with 'lifted up'. The promise that Jesus will be 'lifted up' first appears with a comparison to the brazen serpent lifted up onto a standard during the wanderings of Israel in the desert to cure the people of their sickness (3:14). So, in a way intelligible only to the reader, not to Nicodemus who is present, the son of man is to bring life by being lifted up. But does this mean only that Jesus will be lifted up onto the cross, or does it mean more? The reader cannot be unaware that this same expression is used in the early Christian *kerygma* to mean 'exalted to heaven' at the right hand of God (Acts 2:33; 5:31) with allusion to the messianic Psalm 110. This is the climax both of Peter's speech at Pentecost and of the well-known early Christian hymn quoted by Paul in Philippians 2:6–11.

Again, during the controversy with the Jews in the Temple that leads to attempts to stone Jesus for blasphemy, this mysterious lifting up is to be the occasion when they will recognise his divinity: 'When you have lifted up the son of man, then you will know that I am he' (8:28). We have already almost reached the statements in the High Priestly prayer in which Jesus explains that his coming Passion will be the occasion for his glorification and the revelation of the fullness of God's love (17:1–6). A third time this 'lifting up' appears, '"When I am lifted up from the earth, I shall draw all people to myself." By these words he indicated the kind of death he would die' (12:32). To the crowd at the festival it can hardly indicate the kind of death he would die. Only to a prescient reader, knowing the outcome, is it a prophecy of the Passion and redemption.

Nor are these mysterious expressions the only presages of the coming Passion. Ominous allusions are scattered throughout the gospel, forming a backcloth which protrudes through the rest of the scenery and prepares the reader for the final climax. At Jesus' very first appearance, in the Jordan Valley where John was baptising, John hails him as 'the Lamb of God' as though this title makes perfect sense to his followers to whom he is speaking. To the reader, however, it does make sense, in view of the final identification of Jesus with the Passover lambs, slaughtered at the same time as he dies on the cross, and with the Suffering Servant of the Lord, led like a lamb to the slaughter-house (Isaiah 53:7). At the cleansing of the Temple Jesus almost challenges the Jews with his imperative, 'Destroy this Temple and in three days I will raise it up' (John 2:19), especially as the evangelist makes clear that the Temple is his body, and that he is referring to his Death and Resurrection. The murderous opposition of the Jewish leaders is constant: 'But that only made the Jews more intent on killing him' (5:18). The hostility surrounding Jesus and his activity becomes especially palpable when he is planning to go up to the Festival of Shelters: 'He could not travel round Judaea because the Jews were seeking to kill him' (7:1 and the whole of 7:1–27). The confrontation between Jesus and 'the Jews' becomes tenser as he reveals his claims: 'At this they picked up stones to throw at him' (8:59, cf. 10:31), even before the final decision provoked by the amazement at the raising of Lazarus (11:53). The sole parable of this gospel, the Good Shepherd (10:7–18), centres on the sacrificial death of Jesus – in defiance of good farming principles, for it is surely not good husbandry that a shepherd should die to save any particular sheep.

CONCLUSION

The importance of this sketch is that it shows how, in each of the gospels, the future events of the Passion are already in view during the account of Jesus' ministry, and how the expectation of the Passion influences that account. This certainly does not mean that history has been falsified to accommodate later events. On the other hand, events take on quite new significance if they are seen as part of a pattern: incidents, controversies, sayings take on a new dimension if they are seen to be a prelude to the Passion. The sketch also provides a suggestion that the accounts of the Passion will themselves be shaped to bring out their significance as part of a pattern. The historian will surely describe an event differently if it is seen as a world-shaking and world-forming event, rather than a single incident, however tragic, in the life of an individual.

In order to appreciate the theological orientation of the evangelists it is well to try to discern the historical process as it would be seen by an author interested only in the politico-historical dimension of events. This will enable us to see in what way and to what extent the gospel accounts have developed and expressed a point of view which would not be related by a politico-military historian.

Seeing the black-and-white uncoloured outline of a picture can help to appreciate its colour. The analogy is not quite exact, for, as we said earlier, every historian selects and constructs the picture according to some preconceptions, but it will serve as a rough image.

2

POLITICO-HISTORICAL BACKGROUND TO THE EXECUTION OF JESUS

Before the examination of the gospel narratives of the Passion two other essential background matters must be examined. First, there is no reasonable historical doubt that Jesus was crucified. Secondly, certain aspects of the political situation of Palestine at this time must be examined, since they form the background to the drama, or rather provide the pieces which come into play.

THE CRUCIFIXION OF JESUS A HISTORICAL FACT

The fullest early outside evidence for Jesus, meagre but significant, comes from the Jewish historian Josephus, writing in the last two decades of the first century. On many subjects he is biased and distorted, but there is no reason to suppose that two of these three passages are inaccurate.

In *The Antiquities of the Jews* (18.5.2) Josephus has a fairly full paragraph on John the Baptist, 'who was a good man and commanded the Jews to exercise virtue, both as to righteousness towards one another and piety towards God, and so to come to baptism, because the washing would be acceptable to God'. Herod Antipas arrested him in case he should raise a rebellion among the people, 'for they seemed ready to do anything he should advise'. Josephus includes this fact because the subsequent defeat of Herod's army was attributed by many Jews to divine judgement for this action. This slightly more serious analysis than the popular version of John's death given by Mark and Matthew is valuable. It shows that John's influence and baptism was still remembered over half a century later. About Jesus himself, of course, it says nothing.

One mention of Jesus is merely in passing, which makes it all the more persuasive. He adds to the account of the stoning of James in AD 62 that he was 'the brother of Jesus who was called Christ' (*Antiquities*, 20.9.1). So Josephus accepts that at least some people claimed Jesus to be the Messiah. The other mention of Jesus is more important and also more controversial. The text we now have in Josephus is generally accepted to have been expanded by Christian writers in an easily detectable way:

> Now there was about this time Jesus, a wise man, *if it is right to call him a man*, for he accomplished surprising feats – a teacher of such men as receive truth with pleasure. He won over both many Jews and many Greeks. *He was the Christ; and* when Pilate, at the suggestion of the principal men amongst us, had condemned him to the cross, those that loved him at the first did not forsake him*, for he appeared to them alive again the third day, as the divine prophets had foretold these and ten thousand other wonderful things concerning him*. And the tribe of Christians, so named from him, are not extinct at this day (*Antiquities*, 18.3.3).

The probable insertions are indicated by italics. The first is a thinly-veiled claim for his divinity, the second a clear claim that he was the Messiah,[1] and the third an acknowledgement of the Resurrection appearances in accordance with the scriptures. None of these would have been made by Josephus himself.

There is, however, no reason to suppose that the crucifixion was added to Josephus' original text. Whatever the significance seen by Christians after the event, there is no reason to suppose that the crucifixion of Jesus was other than a dreary, routine event. Crucifixion was

---

[1] And Origen, who quotes this book of Josephus' work five times, twice states that Josephus did not accept Jesus as Messiah (*Comm in Mt 10.17*; *Cels* 1.47). Louis Feldman (*Anchor Bible Dictionary*, 3.991) points out that there are 16 Christian writers in the first four centuries who knew Josephus' works and yet did not mention this passage, which would have been a strong weapon in controversy, especially against the Jews.

a dreadful punishment, which chilled even the brutal Romans. Cicero, admittedly in a rhetorical passage where he is accusing a provincial governor of illegally crucifying a Roman citizen, calls it (*In Verrem* 2.5.165, 169) a *crudelissimum taeterrimumque supplicium* ('a most cruel and disgusting punishment'), and *servitutis extremum summumque supplicium* ('the extreme and ultimate punishment of slavery'). To crucify a Roman citizen was an unspeakable offence, but as a death for recalcitrant slaves and provincials it was nothing remarkable. After the slave-revolt of Spartacus 6,000 slaves were crucified beside the roads as a deterrent to others (Appian, *Bellum Civile*, 1.120), and during the Jewish Revolt escapees from the besieged Jerusalem were sadistically nailed up in the sight of the defenders until there was no room left on the trees of the Mount of Olives (Josephus, *Bellum Judaicum*, 5.451). At the time the crucifixion of Jesus would therefore merit no mention by the historians. The passing reference by the Roman historian Tacitus half a century later is all the more convincing. He is explaining the origin of the Christians to whom Nero attributed the Great Fire of Rome: 'The initiator of this group, Christ, was executed during the reign of Tiberius by the procurator Pontius Pilate' (*Annals*, 15.44).

THE GOVERNANCE OF JUDAEA IN THE TIME OF JESUS

After the death of Herod the Great in 4 BC his kingdom was divided between his four surviving sons, known as the 'tetrarchs' ('rulers of a quarter'). The southern-western and most important quarter, Judaea, Samaria and Idumea, was allotted to Archelaus. He proudly stamped his coins with the title 'ethnarch' ('ruler of the race'), which implies that he was the principal of the four. His incompetence and savagery were, however, legendary, and after a stormy ten years he was summoned to Rome by Augustus, deposed and exiled to Vienne in Gaul.[2] As this action shows, the Herods were client-princes, licensed, so to

---

[2] Alternatively, the reason for Archelaus' removal could have been dynastic intrigue between the sons of King Herod. This, together with a desire for the financial gain of taxation going direct to Rome, may be the reason why Augustus imposed direct rule rather than giving the territory to one of Herod's other sons. See Bond, 1998, p. 4.

speak, by Rome and ultimately under the control of the Emperor. This was normally considered a transitional stage, and the task of the client-prince was to civilise (i.e. Romanise) his territory for eventual incorporation into the Empire as a province.

Archelaus' territory was then subjected to direct Roman rule. Most of the territory of the Roman Empire was governed by senators, very senior administrators of Rome. There was a clearly defined career path in Roman politics, the *cursus honorum*. After a decade of military service a young man (usually from a good family) could enter politics. He would then work his way up the ladder through election to various magistracies in Rome; aedile, praetor and finally consul. There had to be at least a two-year gap between these offices. In the intervening years between holding them, the magistrate would normally exercise office – and increase his experience – by holding a similar post in the provinces of the Empire. Ex-magistrates not so employed composed the Senate, which had once – before the institution of the imperial role by Julius Caesar and Augustus – been the supreme ruling body of the Roman state. The pro-praetor or pro-consul who finally governed a province was therefore a senior official of considerable administrative experience. He was appointed to the post either by the Emperor or by the Senate, for there was a delicate balance of power between the two.

Judaea was not made a province under the rule of a Roman magistrate or ex-magistrate, a member of the Senate. Instead, it enjoyed the same status as several smaller territories, such as Sardinia or the Alps, or Egypt, the bread-basket of the Roman Empire. These were ruled by an employee of the Emperor, a man of lower status and responsible directly to him. Such a prefect or procurator had not worked his way up the administrative ladder, the *cursus honorum*, of offices at home and abroad, but could have entered the imperial service in a quite different way. Quite often such powerful – and normally very capable – officials had started their career as slaves of the Emperor. At a certain stage they would be granted their freedom, but still remain closely dependent on the Emperor as his personal 'freedmen'. In fact, during the latter part of the Emperor Tiberius' reign, much of the administration of the Empire as a whole was left in the hands of a shady and unpopular freedman called Sejanus. The prefect had in principle the same powers as a senatorial governor.[3] However, in the case of Judaea, the senatorial governor of the neighbouring province of Syria seems to have had a sort of vague oversight and could intervene if necessary. One instance of such intervention occurred when Pilate was felt to have reacted too sharply in AD 36 to a messianic revolt in Samaria. The governor of Syria intervened and sent Pilate off to Rome to explain himself to the Emperor. But the Emperor died and Pilate never returned. We do not know whether he was censured at Rome, or whether, after an unusually long tenure of office in Judaea, he was simply given another appointment.

It would, however, be a mistake to imagine Rome as an occupying power, in the same sense as England occupying India or Russia occupying Poland – British soldiers or KGB men everywhere, answerable to ubiquitous District Commissioners or Kommissars. The Roman principle everywhere in its vast Empire was to leave as much as possible of the government to the natives. Roman rule did not replace the local government, but rather was superimposed on it, so that the standard work can state that the governors 'were there to fight Rome's wars, collect Rome's taxes and exercise such supervision of the socii as was necessary for the security of Rome, Romans living in the provinces and the socii themselves' (Lintott, 1993, p. 54). The governor, whether prefect or senator, did not have a large staff and certainly no permanent bureaucracy. His staff was small, strictly personal, selected by himself, and both brought out and returning to Rome with him. Details of how the government functioned were determined by the edict worked out by each governor on his appointment, though of course a wise governor would learn from his predecessors and would take over much of a predecessor's edict. The governor had certain specific tasks:

1. To keep the peace both externally and internally. That this was conceived as the primary task for the early governors of Judaea is suggested by their title, *praefectus*, a military title. Only from AD 44 were they given the more civilian and fiscal title *procurator*. The size of the forces available for this task varied from province to province. The governor of Judaea, a small territory, not on the border of the Empire, had few troops at his command, no legions but only

---

[3] See discussion in chapter 1 of Sherwin-White, 1963.

auxiliaries. They were garrisoned at his capital, the coastal city of Caesarea, and in the Antonia Fortress at Jerusalem. It was primarily to prevent public disorder that the governor would go up to Jerusalem for the three great pilgrimage festivals, when huge crowds would gather, and when nationalistic fervour might assert itself.

2. To ensure the collection of taxes for Rome. This was of vital importance in Roman eyes, and it is hardly an exaggeration to say that in this period the Roman powers regarded the Empire principally as a source of enrichment to themselves. The Emperor Tiberius was known for keeping men in office for a long period. Josephus was of the opinion (*Antiquities*, 18.6.172–177) that one reason why Tiberius in a reign of 22 years appointed only two governors of Judaea was that each governor would milk the provincials to enrich himself, but each would do so only once. Fewer governors, less embezzlement.

3. To oversee the administration of certain cases of justice. On the whole Roman magistrates were cavalier in their treatment of provincials, though they had to be considerably more careful in cases involving Roman citizens. Theoretically provincials had no rights, and could be punished summarily, though obviously such behaviour, unmitigated, would not make for a peaceful or happy province. Scholars continue to be divided on whether the death penalty was reserved for the Roman authority, or whether local courts had this right. Helen K. Bond has a neat footnote (p. 16) on the matter, pointing out that there was at least one case in which the Jews could execute even a Roman citizen, namely trespass on the sanctuary of the Temple (Josephus, *Bellum Judaicum*, 6.4.125). The statement in John 18:31, and the presumption throughout the Passion Narratives, that only the governor has authority to impose the death penalty, is often treated as 'theologically motivated'. The only useful legal evidence is provided by an imperial decree for Cyrene, the so-called Cyrene Edict No 4: 'This does not apply to capital charges, which whoever holds the eparchy (ἐπαρχήν) must hear and decide personally'.[4] The whole question is therefore whether a decree made for a similar territory in Africa has probative value for the governance of Judaea. It will be clear by now that the threat of violence or

---

[4] Ehrenberg and Jones, 1955, no. 311.

nationalist disturbance during the Passover festival was just the sort
of charge to which a governor could be expected to react forcefully.

Apart from these tasks government was carried on by the regime which
had existed before the Roman take-over. In the case of Judaea this
constituted a major difficulty: Herod the Great, in his anxiety to eliminate all possible rivals, had ruthlessly suppressed dignitaries and
notables who could be regarded as a danger (e.g. Josephus, *Antiquities*,
15.7.266). Indeed his elimination of his own family at the slightest
suggestion of rivalry prompted his friend the Emperor Augustus to the
Greek pun that he would rather be Herod's pig than his son (*huios*,
'son', *hus,* 'pig'). As his own death approached, in an attempt to ensure
that there was due mourning in the land, Herod gathered all the notables
of the land into the theatre at Jericho and ordered that when he died
they too should be slaughtered (Josephus, *Antiquities*, 17.6.178), an
order never carried out. All his officials except the High Priest were
his own creation, dependent entirely on him. High Priests themselves
were allowed to remain in office for an average of only four years,
which prevented them becoming an independent threat.[5] When the
Romans therefore removed Judaea from the control of Herod's family
it was natural that government should revert to the High Priest. The
priest appointed in AD 6 was Ananus ben Sethi, whose family had
hitherto been unknown, but who was to become the lynchpin of a high-
priestly dynasty, for five of his sons and his son-in-law Caiaphas were
to become High Priests. Until the end of Herod's reign, however, the
High Priest was continuously kept in check by the device of the governor retaining control of the vestments he needed to perform his
functions. The High Priest, therefore, could not exercise his office fully
unless he remained on the right side of the governor. It must also be
noted that the High Priest's residence was immediately adjacent to the
governor's residence at Jerusalem in the Citadel; may one assume that
during their ten years of shared office they will have met or even dined
together fairly frequently? It is possible that Vitellius' dismissal of

---

[5] Goodman, 1987, pp. 40–44. It is an important thesis of the author's book that the
reason for the chaos which eventually led to the Jewish Revolt in AD 66 was
the lack of competent and respected leadership, and the consequent factional
bickering.

Caiaphas at the same time as Pilate was grounded in a close association of the two.

In his tasks the High Priest was assisted by others. The conventional picture is that there was a body called 'the Sanhedrin', though the exact function, status and composition of this body remains a matter of controversy. E. P. Sanders points out that 'this general consensus rests on a harmonisation of Josephus, the gospels and the Talmud'.[6] The Great Sanhedrin eventually became the ruling body in Judaism, and it is easy to read the situation back from the Talmud into the time of Jesus five hundred years earlier. Martin Goodman cautions that 'all assertions about the function and composition of the Sanhedrin are fraught with problems because of a radical conflict between the evidence of the rabbinic sources of the second century AD and later and that of the New Testament' (p. 113). On two occasions Josephus gives different accounts in different works: in *The Jewish War* he mentions a group of councillors round the king, but in *The Antiquities of the Jews* (written in 93/94, some 20 years later, when the rabbis, gathered at Yavneh, had already begun to have some authoritative power) calls them the Sanhedrin (*Bellum Judaicum*, 1.208–11 cf. *Antiquities*, 14.177; *Bellum Judaicum*, 1.434, cf. *Antiquities*, 15.1723). However, both these occasions describe incidents before the reign of Herod the Great, nearly a century before the events of the Passion. Even if the Sanhedrin existed before Herod's reign, it is unlikely that the autocratic Herod would have left it in place or brooked the restrictive powers of such a council. Nor in fact is there any sign of it in the historical records. The situation is obviously much more fluid than is normally supposed. Sanders[7] gives a significant summary of Josephus' account of the events in Jerusalem leading up to the outbreak of war in AD 66, where the leading parties are described variously as 'the chief priests', 'the powerful', 'the best known men'. Only once (*Bellum Judaicum*, 2.331) is a report to the council (βουλή) mentioned. This suggests that there was at most an informal body of respected men.

In evaluating the New Testament evidence it is important to note three separate uses of the term 'sanhedrin':

---

[6] Sanders, 1985, p. 312.
[7] Sanders, 1985, p. 314–15).

1. 'They will deliver you to sanhedrins' (Mark 13:9/Matt. 10:17). These are some sort of local bodies, perhaps reflecting the councils of elders which ruled the Jewish communities of the Diaspora.
2. 'The chief priests and the Pharisees called *a* sanhedrin' (John 11:47), that is, a meeting. This is the sole occurrence of the term in John. Should Luke 22:66 be included in the same sense, 'Jesus was brought into their *meeting*', or should it be the place, '*meeting-hall*'?
3. The body before which are arraigned Jesus (Mark 14:55; 15:1; Matt. 26:59; Luke 22:66) and the early followers of Jesus in Acts 4–6. Whether the body mentioned at the arraignment of Jesus is an official law court, let alone a constitutional body, remains very dubious. It could equally well have been an informal gathering of elders. On the other hand, the body to which the tribune delivers Paul in Acts 22:30–23:9, 'the chief priests and the entire Sanhedrin' does seem to be firmer and more formal.

There is no reason to suppose that the machinery and bodies of a modern democracy or constitutional monarchy existed. In Josephus as in the New Testament it is clear that the High Priest was in control of day-to-day affairs in Judaea, with an informal group of 'chief priests' to back him up. The fullest recent studies conclude that there was no such thing as 'a permanent institution, let alone a "representative body"'.[8]

The difficulty is to explain the different situation which seems to have existed as a background to Acts and later. At the beginning of the Jewish War Josephus wrote from Galilee to the Sanhedrin for instructions and was given them (*Vita*, 62). As early as AD 62 he reports that the High Priest Ananus 'assembled the Sanhedrin of judges' to try James the brother of Jesus (*Antiquities*, 20.200). The clue may lie in the restoration of direct Roman rule after the death of Agrippa in AD 44. Josephus reports in *The Jewish War*, 2.220: 'Claudius made the country a Roman province and sent Cuspius Fadus to be its procurator, and after him Tiberius Alexander, who, making no alterations of the ancient laws, kept the nation in tranquillity.' It was at this time that the title of

---

[8] McLaren, 1991, p. 223; Nodet, 2002, p. 41: 'On peut conclure fermement non seulement que la séance du Sanhédrin est intrusive, mais surtout que l'institution elle-même l'est'.

the Roman governor was changed from *praefectus* to *procurator*, the sign of a more settled and permanent form of government. Was it also at this stage that a Sanhedrin was given some formal role, which role is to some extent read back by the New Testament writers into the earlier situation?

PILATE'S GOVERNORSHIP OF JUDAEA

It has long been standard practice to represent Pontius Pilate as a monster. The difficulties about this are double. Firstly, there is a contradiction: his rule in general is seen as inhumanly cruel and unyielding, while at the same time his conduct at the trial of Jesus is represented as weak, in that although he repeatedly declared Jesus innocent, he finally condemned Jesus to an unjust death. Is it plausible that the same man could display such contrary characteristics? Secondly, the extra-biblical sources responsible for the denigration of the governor are so patently arguing from their own political motivations that a sound source-criticism casts heavy doubt on their presentation of the evidence. I first raised this question in an obscure little article, 'Suffered under Pontius Pilate' in *Scripture* 18 (1966), pp. 84–93. The matter was taken up by B. C. McGing, 'Pontius Pilate and the Sources' in *CBQ* 53 (1991), pp. 416–38,[9] and followed by the magisterial treatment of his doctoral student, Helen K. Bond, in Bond, 1998.

THE EVIDENCE OF PHILO

The extra-biblical sources about Pilate are delicate to handle, being highly rhetorical and slanted to prove their author's point about relationship between Judaism and Rome. The earliest witness is Philo, who gives a highly coloured account of a single incident in Pilate's tenure of office:

> With the intention of annoying the Jews rather than of honouring Tiberius, he set up gilded shields in Herod's palace in the Holy

---

[9] Whether I can claim any paternity for Professor McGing's views can no longer be established. I gave him a lecture on the subject about the time of the publication of my article, when he was my secondary-school pupil at Ampleforth.

City. They bore no figure and nothing else that was forbidden, apart from the bare inscription which stated two things, the name of the dedicator and that of the person in whose honour the dedication was made. (*Legatio ad Gaium*, #299)

Writing less than ten years after Pilate's term of office ended, Philo should be well in control of the facts, but his presentation of them is suspect on several grounds:

1. Philo's presentation of history here and throughout this work is typical of the genre of 'pathetic history', seen also in the Book of Esther and Second Maccabees. Motives are freely and groundlessly attributed to the actors according to whether the author approves of them or not. Those who favour the Jews always end up doing well, and their opponents are visited by dreadful punishments.

2. The character traits ascribed to Pilate, 'who was a man of inflexible, stubborn and cruel disposition' (#301) and indulged in 'venality, violence, thefts, assaults, abusive behaviour, frequent executions of untried prisoners and endless savage ferocity' (#302), are stock traits regularly ascribed by Philo to other officials whom he reckoned to be enemies of the Jews (see McGing, 1991, p. 432–3; Bond, 1998, p. 31).

3. The motive of annoying the Jews is implausible in itself, granted that the shields were on the inside rather than outside of the palace, and especially in view of the fact that they 'bore no figure and nothing else that was forbidden apart from' the barest inscription. Pilate would normally have put up a statue, which would have been offensive, going against the prohibition of graven images. However, the normal entitulature of the emperor, *divus, divi filius, pontifex maximus* ('god, son of a god, High Priest') was presumably quite enough to be offensive. The Jews objected to any divine title being given to anyone other than God, especially in God's own holy city. The rivalry suggested by *pontifex maximus* may also have riled the High Priest. Nevertheless, far from being provocative, it could be argued that Pilate was carefully tactful, limiting his honour for the emperor to an *aniconic* inscription on the *inside* walls of the palace.

The purpose of Philo's letter was to dissuade Gaius from setting up an equestrian statue of himself in the Temple. In this context, the purpose of the story, in a letter to Tiberius' grandson, was of course to give Gaius a model to follow: far from setting up a statue of himself, Tiberius had had an honorific inscription of himself, and a relatively inoffensive one at that, removed from Jerusalem. So the chief motivation for including the incident was to highlight a contrast between Pilate and Tiberius. This becomes clear immediately afterwards. When Tiberius receives a letter of complaint from the Jewish officials,

> It would be superfluous to describe his anger, although he was not easily moved to anger, since his reaction speaks for itself! For immediately, without even waiting until the next day, he wrote to Pilate, reproaching and rebuking him a thousand times for his new-fangled audacity and telling him to remove the shields at once (#304–5).

So Tiberius is represented as the noble, considerate and sensitive Roman, while Pilate is demonised as the sacrilegious and deliberately provocative petty official.

THE EVIDENCE OF JOSEPHUS

If the one piece of superficially damaging evidence produced by Philo may also be interpreted to show Pilate's care not to offend the Jews, is the evidence given by Josephus, some decades later, any more damning? In *The Jewish War* (2.169–177) Josephus relates two incidents involving Pilate. But, as Helen Bond points out (pp. 50–57), his purpose is not to blacken Pilate but to demonstrate his thesis – one of the main themes of the work – that respectful and peaceful protest can achieve its object, while violent resistance to the might of Rome is useless or counterproductive. 'The emphasis is not so much on Pilate's *initial action* as the Jewish *reaction* and what effect this produces on the Roman prefect' (p. 55). In the first incident peaceful protest achieves its objective; in the second violent resistance leads only to bloodshed. Josephus stresses elsewhere in the work the astonishing devotion of the Jews to their Law, and the effect which it has in swaying the Roman authorities (1.148 on Pompey; 2.195–198 on Petronius; 2.236–244 under Cumanus' governorship; 7.406 at Masada).

Pilate, being sent by Tiberius as procurator to Judaea, in an under-hand way introduced into Jerusalem under cover of night the images of Caesar which are called standards. This proceeding, when day broke, aroused immense excitement among the Jews; those on the spot were in consternation, considering their laws to have been trampled under foot, as those laws permit no image to be erected in the city, while at this indignation of the townsfolk the country people flocked together as one body. Hastening to Pilate at Caesarea, the Jews implored him to remove the standards from Jerusalem and to observe their ancestral customs. When Pilate refused, they fell prostrate around his house and for five whole days and nights remained motionless in that position.

On the ensuing day Pilate took his seat on his tribunal in the great stadium and summoning the multitude, on the pretext of giving them an answer, gave the arranged signal to his soldiers to surround the Jews with a ring of weapons. Finding themselves surrounded by troops three deep, the Jews were struck dumb at this unexpected sight. Pilate announced that he would cut them down if they refused to admit Caesar's images, and signalled to the soldiers to draw their swords. Thereupon the Jews, as by concerted action, flung themselves in a body on the ground, extended their necks, and shouted that they were ready rather to die than to transgress the Law. Overcome with astonishment at such intense religious zeal, Pilate gave orders for the immediate removal of the standards from Jerusalem.

On a later occasion he provoked a fresh uproar by expending upon the construction of an aqueduct all the sacred treasure known as Korbonas; the water was brought from a distance of 400 fur-longs. Indignant at this, the populace formed a ring round the tribunal of Pilate, then on a visit to Jerusalem, and continuously shouted him down. He, foreseeing their tumult, had interspersed among the crowd a troop of his soldiers, armed but disguised in civilian dress, with orders not to use their swords, but to beat with cudgels those who had been shouting. He now from his tribunal gave the agreed signal. Large numbers of the Jews perished, some from the blows, others trodden to death in the flight by their companions. Cowed by the fate of the victims, the multitude was reduced to silence. (based on Loeb translation)

The sudden introduction of these two incidents (the previous three decades of Roman rule having been passed over without comment), and their position before similar instances of the effect of Jewish piety on the Romans, makes it clear that this, rather than any interest in Pilate for himself, is the centre of Josephus' focus. It is, however, possible also to hazard some deductions about Pilate's character.

There is no suggestion that Pilate was acting out of cruelty or malice, just that two of his actions upset his subjects. The former was an offence against their sensitivities to the Law. It is, however, quite possible that Pilate's introduction of the iconic standards by night was precisely an attempt to avoid upsetting the Jews in Jerusalem: army regulations would be obeyed by following the standards[10] and the Jews would not see the standards as the troops marched into the city. He blusters and threatens, but in the end yields diplomatically. The latter incident is simply a protest against overspending. The complicated piece of engineering[11] must have increased significantly the water-supply to Jerusalem at a time when the population was expanding; its construction suggests serious and prolonged co-operation between the Roman and Jewish authorities. The protest was only against the excessive cost, which *used up* the sacred funds (ἐξαναλίσκων). Perhaps it ran over budget. But again, in attempting to avoid bloodshed by controlling the crowd through plain-clothes policemen with truncheons, Pilate showed tact, resourcefulness and consideration. In the end things got out of hand.

Twenty years later, however, Josephus gives a somewhat different account of Pilate's activity in his *Antiquities of the Jews*. Again, his interest is not primarily in Pilate. He recounts the incidents as part of the worsening relationships between Rome and the Jews, which will

---

[10] And the importance of strict adherence to army rules is obvious to anyone who has seen the identical design of Roman camps (even to the positioning of the latrines) at Housesteads on Hadrian's Wall and at Masada on the shore of the Dead Sea.

[11] There is a plethora of aqueducts leading to Jerusalem. J. Wilkinson (*Palestine Exploration Quarterly*, 1974, p. 46) guesses that Pilate's is the so-called high-level aqueduct into Jerusalem. A. Mazar in Dierx and Garbrecht 2001, pp. 165–94), however, deduces from inscriptions of the X Legion (stationed in Palestine in the second century AD) that this channel is later. Since the so-called Arrub Channel, leading into the Pools of Solomon, is 39km long, this corresponds most exactly to Josephus' figure of 400 furlongs.

eventually result in the rebellion of AD 66. In recounting the incident
of the standards Josephus is here at pains to stress that the introduction of the iconic standards was a total novelty deliberately engineered
'in order to abolish the Jewish laws' (18.55). Similarly, in the incident
of the aqueduct he omits the telling detail of the excessive expense of
the aqueduct, and simply broadens the objection to 'the Jews were not
pleased with what had been done' (18.60), removing the suggestion
that the operation began with a certain amount of co-operation. That
his purpose is not primarily to blacken Pilate is shown by the insertion
of two indications that Pilate and his soldiers were provoked to react
to the demonstration: 'Some too even hurled insults and abuse of the
sort that a throng will commonly engage in . . . When the Jews were
in full torrent of abuse he gave his soldiers the prearranged signal'
(18.60–61).

Even in the third incident, the suppression of a messianic uprising
in Samaria, which eventually led to Pilate being packed off to Rome,
Pilate's behaviour was not outrageous. Josephus describes the events,

> [The armed enthusiasts] posted themselves in a certain village
> named Tirathana, and, as they planned to climb the mountain in a
> great multitude, they welcomed to their ranks new arrivals who
> kept coming. But before they could ascend, Pilate blocked their
> projected route up the mountain with a troop of cavalry and
> heavy-armed infantry, who in a confrontation with those who had
> gathered in the village slew some and put the others to flight.
> Many prisoners were taken, of whom Pilate put to death the
> ringleaders and those who were most influential among the fugi-
> tives. (18.87 – based on Loeb translation)

The Samaritans appealed to Vitellius, the legate of Syria, complaining
that 'it was not as rebels against the Romans but as refugees from the
persecution of Pilate that they had met in Tirathana'. Whereupon Vitellius sent one of his staff to look after Judaea and packed Pilate off to
Rome 'to give the Emperor an account of the matters with which he
was charged by the Samaritans' (18.89). It is quite striking that Josephus
deliberately refrains from taking sides himself in the matter, not sup-
porting either the general charge of persecution by Pilate or the
particular charge of excessive severity. Pilate did not return, but by
the time he reached Rome the Emperor was dead, and it may well have

been judged that his unusually long tenure of office in Judaea should at last come to an end. Vitellius himself proceeded into Jerusalem, and there generously revoked the long-standing practice (dating from the time of Herod the Great) that the secular ruler should retain custody of the High Priest's vestments until a week before the three great festivals (18.90, see p. 34) – a useful check on good behaviour. It must particularly have irked the High Priests that the vestments were in the custody of gentiles, and therefore needed to be purified. Vitellius' conciliatory gesture must have stored up considerable goodwill.

This statesmanlike gesture of Vitellius might be seen to contrast with Pilate's failure to understand the Jews. It would support the possibility, suggested by Martin Goodman,[12] that Roman governors of Judaea were unlikely to have been of very high quality. It is possible to see the governors of Judaea as mere puppets, incapable men watched over by the experienced and senior senatorial governor of Syria. Josephus, after all, says that on the death of Archelaus Judaea became a προσθήκη of Syria (*Antiquities*, 18.1.1). This could be understood to mean 'annexe', and in fact the governor of Syria intervened several times in the affairs of Judaea (*Antiquities*, 18.18; 18.261; 20.7; 20.118), at least on the final occasion overruling the governor. How much previous experience Pilate had had we cannot know. A later governor of Judaea, Felix, was a freedman of the Emperor, about whom the aristocratic and sardonic Tacitus remarks *ius regium servili ingenio exercuit* (*Histories*, 5.9, 'with the temperament of a slave he exercised the right of kings'). It was his misgovernment which finally provoked the outbreak of the Jewish Revolt.[13] True, such men had not risen through the testing system of the *cursus honorum*, but were the personal agents of the Emperor, or in the case of Pilate, probably of the Emperor's detested and all-powerful freedman, Sejanus, who handled virtually all the imperial administration until his fall in AD 31. As governors they were hardly entrusted with an independent command. They had no legionary troops but only auxiliaries. It is not surprising that such a person should occasionally make a misjudgement in complicated matters, should feel unsure of himself and allow himself to be manipulated, or should err

---

[12] Goodman, 1987, p. 7–8.
[13] See Schürer, 1973, Vol. 1, pp. 460–64.

on the side of loyalty to his master the Emperor. Was this the case in Pilate's treatment of Jesus?

THE EVIDENCE OF INSCRIPTIONS

So far we have attempted to understand Pilate from the literary sources. Archaeology may also tell us something of the man and his rule. In fact archaeology has so far given us only two traces. One is the solitary inscription recording his name, found at Caesarea, and reading:

>]S TIBERIEVM[14]
>]NTIVS PILATVS
>]ECTVS IVDAE

This presumably commemorates either the building or the repair of a building (it is impossible to establish which building or what type of building) in honour of the emperor Tiberius. At least it shows that Pilate was anxious to honour the emperor.

The other possible archaeological source of information is Pilate's coinage. It has frequently been suggested that these were deliberately provocative, since they incorporated pagan symbols, and even religious symbols. Coins in the ancient world, like postage-stamps in the modern world, were a recognised means of propaganda, proclaiming to the world the loyalties, interests or triumphs of the city or authority which issued them. Portraits of rulers, particularly of the Roman Emperor, were normal. Jewish coinage, however, studiously avoided images of living things or people. The sole exception is a single coin of Herod the Great, which does have an eagle.[15] The last of the Hasmonean rulers of Judaea not surprisingly borrowed pagan motifs although these could be understood in a pagan religious sense, the *cornucopia* and the herald's staff often being associated with the god Hermes. The early Roman governors slightly extended this usage by introducing the

---

[14] Bond, 1998 prints this as 'TIBERIÉVM' (pp. 12, 48, 249), but such accents do not exist in Latin. On the original inscription the supposed acute accent looks to me more like a chance cut in the stone than part of a letter. Presumably this stroke occurred when the stone was re-used in a later building project.

[15] Hill, 1914, p. 227.

kantharos or drinking-vessel often used in libations. Pilate was a little more ambitious. Besides the wreath and grapes used often on Jewish coinage, he struck coins bearing a *lituus* (sacred staff) and a *simpulum* (ladle used in drink-offerings). The purpose of this may have been to continue the process of integrating Jewish and Roman culture rather than upsetting the Jews. It is, in any case, questionable how provocative they would have found this.[16] The gospels show that *denarii* bearing the Emperor's head circulated freely in Palestine. Furthermore, the annual Temple Tax itself was paid in Tyrian shekel (probably because it was a notably reliable, unadulterated coinage), despite the fact that all such coins carry the divine image of either Tyche or Melquart, the god of Tyre. If these could be stored in the Temple, the Jews cannot have been so highly sensitive to their designs. If Pilate had intended to provoke the Jews he would have needed to be far more extreme: perhaps an image of the Emperor on coins intended specifically for Judaea would have been offensive.

---

[16] Bond, 1996.

3

THE AGONY
IN THE GARDEN

MARK'S ACCOUNT
Mark 14:32–43

THE MARKAN AUTHORSHIP

In the middle of the twentieth century, when scissors-and-paste theories were popular, a long series of scholars suggested that in the account of the agony in the garden Mark is combining two accounts, e.g. one source is 14:32, 33b, 35, 40, 41, 42a, the other is 14:33a, 34, 36–39.[1] However, the traits of Mark's personal style are unmistakable throughout the narrative. Most noticeable of all is the triple repetition which is such a feature especially of the Passion Narrative (triple prophecy of the Passion; three questions to Jesus at the Jewish investigation; Peter's three denials; Pilate's three assertions of Jesus' innocence; the threefold division of time on Good Friday). Linguistically the passage is so full of Markan characteristics at every level[2] that only the sketchiest of oral sources, or rather suggestions, can lie behind Mark's final composition.

---

[1] Holleran, 1973.

[2] Almost every sentence begins with καὶ, and is couched in the historic present; nine uses of ἔρχομαι in ten verses; impersonal plural, 14:32; ἤρξατο with infinitive, 14:33; pleonastic synonyms 14:33d; double imperatives 14:34, 38, 41, 42; indirect speech repeated in direct speech, 14:35–36; ἵνα without sense of purpose, 14:35; parenthetic translation of Aramaic, 14:36; καὶ, πάλιν, 14:39, 40; pleonastic 14:35b+36, 39b, 41b, 41b+42b (ἰδοὺ παραδίδοται + ἰδοὺ ὁ παραδούς); delayed explanation with γὰρ, 14:40; periphrastic tense 14:40, cf. Cf. Bird, 1973; Elliott, 1993; Neirynck, 1988.

The relationship of the Markan account to two other New Testament texts remains intriguing. It is not surprising that there seems to have been a tradition in early Christianity about Jesus' agonised prayer at the prospect of his Passion. This tradition took various forms. A similar saying occurs in John 12:27–28.

> Now my soul is troubled. What shall I say? Father, save me from this hour? But it is for this very reason that I have come to this hour. Father, glorify your name. A voice came from heaven, 'I have glorified it and will again glorify it'.

The similarities are manifest: distress at the coming Passion, prayer to the Father, mention of the 'hour', acceptance of the Father's will. But the mode is thoroughly Johannine. John portrays the Passion of Jesus not as the moment of Jesus' humiliation but as the hour of his exaltation and glorification. John's Jesus is nevertheless fully human, so that his soul is troubled by the approaching trial (12:27a). However, it is the moment of his glorification and that of his Father (12:28), to which he has looked forward (2:4; 7:30; 8:20) and will look forward (13:1; 16:32). Accordingly, he thrusts aside the thought of praying to be delivered from it. The image of the cup of suffering seen in the synoptic accounts of the prayer in the garden will also be present at Jesus' arrest in the garden (18:11). There again Jesus accepts the cup in an atmosphere of triumph, for it comes at the conclusion of the arrest-scene, where his divinity has shone through by his use of the mysterious divine 'I am he' (18:5, 6, 8) and the awestruck reaction of the arresting-party in falling to the ground.

There are further echoes of the tradition in the Letter to the Hebrews 5:7–8:

> During his life on earth he offered up prayers and supplications, with loud cries and with tears, to the one who was able to save him from death, and, winning a hearing by his reverence, he learnt obedience, son though he was, by his sufferings.

The details of this tradition about Jesus' prayer are almost entirely different from those of the synoptic scene, though again it is centred on the same motifs of prayer in distress and acceptance in obedience to the divine will. It has been judged to have its origin in an early Christian hymn (compare Phil. 2:6–11). This would account for the poetic pleonasms (prayers and supplication, cries and tears – none of these words occurs elsewhere in Hebrews), and the echoes of the prayers of the persecuted just man in the Psalms, especially Psalm 116:1–8. In the 'winning a hearing by his reverence' there may be also a link to the voice from heaven in John 12:28b and perhaps even to the angel in Luke 22:43. It is a valuable testimony to the vigour and variety of early Christian reflection on the Passion.

The integration of Mark's narrative into the earlier part of the gospel is also strong. Not only is the same little group of three disciples chosen to be alone with Jesus as at the Transfiguration, but just as at the Transfiguration Peter 'did not know what to answer' (9:6), so now – and in the same words (slightly ineptly, since no 'answer' was required!) – 'they did not know what to answer' (14:40). The understanding of events is also strikingly increased if the story is read in the context of the eschatological discourse of Mark 13. There, as here, the theme of the impending approach of the eschatological 'hour' of testing and the need to keep awake is heavily underscored. The moment of testing persecution is described in 13:11 as 'that hour', a pregnant phrase recalling the threatening biblical Day of the Lord. The finale of the chapter stresses that no one can tell when it will arrive (13:32), whence the need to keep awake (13:33, 34, 35, 37). This forms the obvious background for the contrast between Jesus, who sees himself confronting the 'hour' (14:35), and the disciples whose persistent inability to keep awake is the hallmark of their failure. A final eschatological note is sounded by Jesus' ἤγγικεν (14:42, 'has drawn near'), a reminiscence of the same word, expressing the arrival of the eschatological reign of God at the opening of his ministry, 'The time is fulfilled and the kingdom of God has drawn near' (1:15).

THE FAILURE OF THE DISCIPLES

The failure of the disciples, so prominent throughout the gospel, comes to a head in the Passion Narrative. In this scene it is perhaps more central than even Jesus' prayer. As possibly with Peter's denials (see below), the contrast between the intensity of the first prayer of Jesus and the flatness of the other two (in 14:39 Mark is content to say 'he prayed saying the same word', and on the third occasion no prayer is given at all) suggests that Mark had sufficient material only for one prayer, and himself spun it out into three for emphasis. On the other hand, Jesus' triple return to the disciples and his reproaches to them are richly described. One important feature may be that, having spoken in the singular to Peter, he then speaks in the plural to all the disciples (14:37, 38). Is he speaking just to the group present in the garden, or to all disciples undergoing temptation?

The importance of the theme of the failing disciples is so great in Mark that the evangelist must intend it to bear on some contemporary situation of his own community. In the first stage of the gospel the presentation of the disciples is reasonably positive: the first four are called and respond immediately and without question (1:16–20). They are called to be with Jesus and to go out and proclaim, with power to expel evil spirits (3:13–15). They are the privileged recipients of the mystery of the kingship (4:11). They are sent out on their mission, which they fulfil (6:12–13) and seem to receive Jesus' congratulations on returning (6:30–31). Yet even at this early stage all is not well. In direct contrast to his previous contrast between insiders who understand the mystery and outsiders who do not, Jesus shows disappointment that they do not understand the parable of the sower and will therefore be incapable of understanding the parables (4:13). In the storm on the lake there is a sharp exchange, the disciples treating Jesus to sarcasm and Jesus replying with the accusation of cowardice (4:38–40). At the first multiplication of loaves they fail to appreciate Jesus' power to solve the difficulty, and douse him with sarcasm, 'Are we supposed to go off and buy . . .?' (6:37) Their failure to understand about the multiplication of loaves is pointed by Mark, using typically Markan double negatives and double question. After the dispute over the tradition of the elders their lack of comprehension is again underlined by the Markan dual phrase, 'Are even you so lacking in understanding? Do you not realise that . . .?' (7:18). Finally in the discussion after the second bread-miracle they still totally fail to understand the situation, again eliciting a Markan double question, 'Do you still not realise nor understand?' (8:17)

After the symbolic healing of the blind man Peter does reach the turning-point of acknowledging that Jesus is the Christ (8:29), but both he and the other disciples fail to understand what this means. So, after each of the three great prophecies of the Passion, the disciples show misunderstanding, and need the lesson of their sharing in their Master's suffering to be reinforced. In 8:32 Peter remonstrates with Jesus, is rebuked as 'Satan', and provokes Jesus' teaching to the disciples about self-denial. In 9:32 the second prophecy is immediately followed by the quarrel about precedence, which Jesus corrects with his teaching on the primacy of service. In 10:35 the third prophecy is followed by the ambitious and self-seeking request of James and John, to which Jesus opposes the same teaching on the primacy of service.

Once the Passion sequence starts, the situation worsens dramatically. First one of the disciples betrays Jesus, immediately after the highest symbol of friendship, sharing the same dish. Then the inner group of disciples falls asleep in the garden three times. The bitterness of this occasion is underlined by the special involvement of precisely those three disciples who had been favoured with special revelation at the Transfiguration (the link is stressed: again in their abashed confusion they 'knew not what to answer'). James and John had also stoutly protested that they could share Jesus' cup (Mark 10:39). Soon they will abandon him at the arrest and flee, despite their promises (14:31 and 50). The height of irony will be reached in the naked flight of the young man (see p. 59): as at the beginning they forsook all to follow Jesus, now one of them forsakes all to get away! Finally comes Peter's denial in the High Priest's hall, despite his assertion of fidelity till death (14:31).

Time and again the other evangelists reduce or remove the criticism of the disciples in Mark: they must have found it inappropriate. So Mark is teaching some lesson strongly. Theodore T. Weeden ('The Heresy that Necessitated Mark's Gospel' in *ZNW* 59 [1968], pp. 145–158) suggested that his purpose was to counter a view of Jesus as a pure miracle-worker, putting no value on his Passion. A variety of other views has been held, but in some way this stress must be related to the difficulty which any disciple of Jesus has in personally taking on board the demand to follow the Master in suffering.

THE PRAYER

On the one hand, there is a firm tradition, expressed both here and in John 12:27–28 and Hebrews 5:7–8, that Jesus struggled in prayer with the prospect of the tortured death that he faced. (How much did he already know? Did he know that Judas had already set the arrest in motion? Did he realise the depths of the hostility of the Temple authorities? Did he know that the Romans were involved?) On the other, there is no reason to suppose that the words which the evangelists give us were heard or passed down from Jesus himself. The prayer as we have it is built from three elements.

1. The Psalms

From the earliest times Christians attempted to make sense of the stunning events of the Passion by seeing what happened as the fulfilment of scripture. So the earliest tradition, taken up and quoted by Paul, asserts that Christ 'died for our sins according to the scriptures' (1 Cor. 15:3). According to the very literalist exegetical frame of mind then current, seen at its clearest in Matthew (e.g. Matt. 27:3–10) and the scriptural exegesis of the Dead Sea Scrolls, this was to be seen and demonstrated not primarily by the fulfilment of the logic and thrust of the scriptures as a whole. In the twenty-first century the view that the rejection of Jesus was the fulfilment of scripture would be shown with broader brushstrokes. It was the climax of human disobedience and blindness to the divine will, as seen from Adam onwards, but more especially in the story of Israel's infidelities down the ages. Jesus' own acceptance of his role is the climactic expression in human form of the love of God revealed throughout the scriptures in the loving forgiveness of God for his people. By contrast, in the first century the way the Passion fulfilled the scriptures was shown in factual correspondence of details of the events to individual passages of scripture. A rough list of the more obvious scriptural allusions would include:

> I will strike the shepherd and the sheep will be scattered (Zech. 13:7).
> Even the bravest of warriors will run away naked (Amos 2:16).
> I am deeply grieved, even to death (Ps. 42:5).
> False witnesses come forward against me (Ps. 35:11).
> Like a sheep dumb before its shearers (Isa. 53:7).
> I have not turned my face away from insults and spitting (Isa 50:6).
> They divide my garments among them, cast lots for my clothes (Ps. 22:18).
> They jeer at me and wag their heads (Ps. 22:7).
> My God, my God, why have you forsaken me? (Ps. 22:1)

Even the dearest of my friends keep their distance (Ps. 38:11).

He was numbered among evil-doers (Isa. 53:12).

Darkness at noon (Amos 5:18).

Hence the detail in the Gethsemane narrative, 'going on a little further' (14:35) may be a reminiscence of the same phrase in Genesis 22:5, intimating that Jesus' sacrifice is a fulfilment of Abraham's sacrifice of his son Isaac. Accordingly, the prayers of Jesus during his Passion are shown to be those of the persecuted Just Man in the psalms: Psalm 42:5 in Mark 14:34; further examples at Mark 15:34; Luke 23:46.

2. The Image of the Cup

This image is used variously in the Bible, sometimes of the cup of divine wrath which the guilty must drink (e.g. Isa. 51:17; Jer. 25:15–16), but also more generally, and frequently in the inter-testamental literature, of the painful cup of death. The usage here should accord with the two earlier uses by Jesus in the gospel, first when he asks the sons of Zebedee whether they are willing to share his cup and to be plunged into the baptism into which he must be plunged (10:38–39). Secondly, the prayer is surely to be understood in continuity with the cup of the new covenant which Jesus shared at the Supper (14:23–24), indicating Jesus' continuing awareness of this dimension of his coming Passion.

3. 'Abba, Father'

For the prayer itself Mark is using or imitating the formulae of early Christian prayer, with the Aramaic *Abba* immediately followed by its Greek translation (ὁ πατήρ). This double formula of a particular Aramaic word, regarded almost as a talisman, occurs elsewhere in the New Testament (1 Cor. 16:22; Rev. 1:7, *maranatha*, meaning either 'Come, Lord!' or 'The Lord is coming'). Jesus' consciousness that God was his Father was treasured by the early community (e.g. Gal. 4:6), and this usage, stemming from Jesus himself, but rare in the synoptic gospels, was greatly extended, especially in John. The unadorned use of *Abba* for God was held by that great scholar Joachim Jeremias (in Jeremias, 1965) to be unique to Jesus. He held that Jesus' contemporaries would use it only in combination with other, more reverent and distant titles (e.g. 'O Lord, father and ruler of my life', Ecclus (Sir.)

23:1; also now 1 QH 9.35–36). He also held that it is the affectionate
child's way of addressing a father, indicating the warmth and intimacy
of that relationship, so 'Daddy'. However, Fitzmyer's detailed study of
Aramaic of the period[3] shows that only after AD 200 did this become
current, and at the time of Jesus 'Abba' was more formal usage, and
young children called their father *Abi* rather than *Abba*. By its use of
'Abba' and by the focus on obedient submission to God's will, Jesus'
prayer already in Mark (and more explicitly, as we shall see, in Matthew)
recalls the atmosphere of early Christian prayer such as the Lord's
Prayer. As elsewhere, Mark uses the triple repetition to emphasise the
intensity of Jesus' prayer.

MATTHEW'S ACCOUNT
Matthew 26:36–46

In Matthew's account, besides many little characteristic verbal changes
of style, three changes of emphasis are visible. Firstly, Matthew tones
down the lurid colours in which Mark paints Jesus' agony of mind: for
Mark's word for Jesus' almost stunned distress (ἐκθαμβεῖσθαι),
Matthew has the more seemly 'grieved'. Instead of Mark's uncontrol-
lable 'falling [repeatedly, if the imperfect is taken seriously, as though
Jesus were simply stumbling and unable to remain on his feet] to the
ground' the biblical attitude of reverent prayer is indicated by 'fell face
to the ground in prayer' (26:39). This is in accord with Matthew's
generally more dignified, and even hieratic, presentation of Jesus.

Secondly Matthew fills out the second prayer of Jesus. After the
Jewish manner of respect for the Lord, both prayers are impersonal:
'let this cup pass from me', instead of Mark's direct request, 'remove
this cup from me'. This grammatical change also enables Matthew to

---

[3] Fitzmyer, 1985. He rejects (p. 27) as valid evidence for the first century the
charming fifth-century version of the story about the first-century Rabbi Honi:
During a drought school children were sent to him to say, 'Father, Father, give us
rain', whereupon Honi prayed, 'Master of the Universe, do it for the sake of these
who are unable to distinguish between the father who gives rain and the father who
does not.' However, the novelty of this address by Jesus in prayer to his Father
still remains. Fitzmyer concludes, 'There is no evidence in the literature of pre-
Christian or first-century Palestinian Judaism that *'abba'* was used in any sense
as a personal address for God by an individual – and for Jesus to address God as
'abba' is therefore something new' (p. 28).

assimilate Jesus' prayer to the Lord's Prayer, which he has set down at
the very centre of the Sermon on the Mount, 'Your will be done' (26:42
as 6:10). It may be presumed that, since Jesus is the model for his
disciples, he will pray the same phrases as he taught them to pray, or
rather *en revanche*, his prayer at this desperate time becomes the model
for the prayer of all disciples in desperation. The intimacy of both first
and second prayers is stressed by the affectionate address, 'My father'
(26:39, 42); this perhaps indicates both similarity and distinction
between Jesus and his disciples, who are instructed to pray with the
plural '*Our* father' (6:9). At the same time, a certain hesitancy is shown –
perhaps the hesitancy of respect – by the repeated '*if* it is possible'
(26:39), '*if* it is not possible' (26:42), instead of Mark's confident 'for
you all things are possible' (14:36). After this elaboration of the second
prayer, Matthew can transfer to the third prayer Mark's minimal account
of the second, 'saying the same word' (Mark 14:39; Matt. 26:44).

Matthew's third concern is to underline the solidarity which exists
between Jesus and his disciples. This is clear from the beginning:
instead of Mark's typical impersonal 'they came', Matthew has '*Jesus*
came *with them*'. As always, he tones down their failure, by omitting
Mark's critical 'they did not know what to say to him' (Mark 14:40).
He also takes the spotlight off Peter by removing Jesus' intimate and
disappointed question to him, 'Simon, are you asleep?' (Mark 14:37),
and by putting into the plural the criticism, 'Could you not stay awake
with me one hour?' (Matthew 26:40). This now concerns not only Peter
but all the disciples. Twice he adds 'with me' to 'stay awake' (26:38,
40); they should share in his Passion, as they frequently do in Matthew.
Jesus' community will benefit from his permanent presence (1:23;
18:20; 28:18–20) and will share in his ministry of forgiveness (9:8;
18:18). To underline still further the unity of Jesus with his disciples
at this moment, where Mark twice has simply 'he came back', Matthew
states explicitly 'he came back *to the disciples*' (26:40, 45). If one
cannot speak of Jesus' emotional dependence on the disciples at this
critical moment, Matthew does at least intimate that he is glad to be
with them.

LUKE'S ACCOUNT
Luke 22:40–46

Luke's version of the scene on the Mount of Olives (there is no mention of 'Gethsemane'; he often omits odd-sounding place-names, and has little interest in the topography of Jerusalem) is drastically shortened and welded into a forceful unity. There is only one prayer and one return to the disciples. It is framed at beginning and end by the command, 'Pray that you may not come into temptation' (22:40, 46), exemplifying once more the Lukan theme of prayer, and more especially of the disciple praying after the model of the Master. In their persecutions and martyrdom, as in their working of miracles, the Acts of the Apostles will show the disciples mirroring exactly and continuing the life of Jesus into the era of the Church. In the Passion Narrative too this carefully painted imitation comes to view in such details as Simon of Cyrene carrying the cross 'behind Jesus' (23:26). All stress has been taken off the failure of the disciples, both by eradication of the triple repetition and by a couple of subtle changes in 22:45: instead of 'sleeping' they are now (despite NRSV) 'lying down from grief', that is, their sympathy with Jesus is so intense that they could not stay on their feet. There is a clear echo of this phrase 'from grief' in the disciples' lack of recognition of the Risen Christ 'from joy' (24:41). Nevertheless, when Jesus firmly 'stands erect' after his prayer he comes to them and tells them too to join him in this confident posture (22:45, 46).

The most notable difference in Luke is the presentation of Jesus himself. Quite definitely, though not yet so emphatically as in John, Jesus is in control of his Passion and Death: he will be arrested only when he has exercised his healing ministry (22:51) and given the arresting party his consent, 'This is your hour' (22:53). He dies only when he has commended his spirit into his Father's hands (23:46). So now, Jesus does not collapse onto the ground, but 'knelt down', as Christians later do in earnest prayer of petition (Acts 7:60; 9:40; 20:36; 21:5). There is no sign of distress: his single prayer is calm and resigned, with the same resignation shown later by Christians (Acts 21:14). But there is nothing lacking in the intensity of his prayer.

The verses 22:43–44 are missing in some manuscripts, but are widely quoted in the second century. If they are considered part of Luke's gospel they contain two features, showing the preparation of Jesus for his Passion. Both have analogies in the Books of Maccabees to which the genre of Luke–Acts is so similar. Firstly, Jesus is represented as an athlete about to enter a contest, with his adrenalin up, rather than terrified and horror-struck as in Mark. There is no question of sweating blood, as piety has often asserted; it is merely that his sweat flowed like blood. This is the physical condition of those preparing for martyrdom in the Books of Maccabees (2 Macc. 3:16; 15:19; 4 Macc. 6:6, 11). Secondly, an angel appears to show that Jesus' prayer is regarded, just as in Mark 1:13 at the earlier testing in the desert, and as two angels came to strengthen Eleazar at his martyrdom. After his prayer Jesus stands confidently upright, and comes to tell his followers to do the same in their prayer during temptation.

4

THE ARREST

The second scene in the garden undergoes considerable development through the gospels, beginning with a little, rather chaotic and puzzling scene in Mark and moving through to a Johannine presentation which is in some ways the key to his Passion Narrative.

MARK'S ACCOUNT – THE BETRAYAL
Mark 14:43–52

Consonant with his consistent emphasis on the failure of the disciples, in Mark all is centred on the betrayal by Judas and the flight of the disciples. This is another instance of Mark's technique of framing for contrast: he frames the account of Jesus' fidelity with that of the infidelity of his followers.

The scene has been prepared firstly by the introduction to the Last Supper (14:17–21). It is easy to read this scene with the emphasis given to it by Matthew 26:20–25, which in fact is subtly different: in Matthew the scene of dipping in the dish leads up in the final verse to the identification of the traitor as Judas. This had been prepared by the question and answer of each of the disciples and Jesus in 26:22–23. By inserting 'This is the one' (οὖτος) into Jesus' answer Matthew indicates that a sort of identity-parade is in progress. In Mark the emphasis is different, concentrating not on the identity of the traitor so much as on the depths of treachery shown by one who has shared a meal, 'he who eats with me' (Mark 14:18, omitted by Matthew). The disciples do not ask, as in Matthew, 'Surely it is not me, Lord?', but merely protest, 'Certainly not me!'. In Mark, accordingly, the scene

ends, 'Better for that man if he had never been born', without the
positive identification given by Matthew. A second preparation has been
given by Mark on the way to Gethsemane, in the form of the scriptural
quotation predicting the flight of all the disciples, 'I shall strike the
shepherd and the sheep will be scattered' (Zech. 13:7), completed by
the prophecy of Peter's desertion and his blustering protestations of
loyalty. The Gethsemane scene then ends with the betrayal of Judas
and the flight of the disciples, leaving Peter's desertion still in the
future.

Betrayal continues as the accent of Mark's description. As soon as
Judas appears his desertion is underlined by 'one of the Twelve', an
expression used three times of Judas, and of him alone (Mark 14:10,
20, 43; Matt. 26:14). The contrast is marked in the next verse: he
betrays Jesus but had shown his solidarity with his captors by working
out an 'agreed sign' with the armed mob. The agreed sign was to be a
kiss, but Judas does not stop at this. He respectfully calls Jesus 'Rabbi'
and gives him an *affectionate* kiss – not φιλέω but καταφιλέω, which
expresses especial warmth, often a caress – and the trap is sprung.

Then follows the first curious episode, one of the bystanders drawing
his sword and cutting off the ear of the servant of the High Priest. Who
are these two, assailant and victim? Matthew 26:51 is precise that the
assailant is 'one of those with Jesus', and John 18:10 will identify him
further as Peter. But there is no hint of this in Mark, and nowhere else in
Mark are the disciples described as οἱ παρεστηκότες (the bystanders).
Furthermore, it is odd that any of them should be armed, though Luke's
addition at the Last Supper, 22:36–38, would permit this. In John 18:10
the servant's name has become Malchus, in accordance with the law of
increasing detail as stories are passed down. It is curious that he is
called '*the* servant of the High Priest', and Ben Viviano[1] has suggested
that he is the servant of the High Priest in an honoured sense of 'right-
hand man' or vizier. The removal of his ear would then disqualify him
from sacred office, according to Leviticus 21:18 LXX, and the incident
can be read as a reflection on the whole Temple cult. The incident is
the more curious, in that in Mark it seems without consequence or
reaction, for Jesus' next statement disregards it and refers back over it

---

[1] Viviano, 1989.

to the unjustified aggressiveness of his captors, when they could have arrested him as he taught in the Temple.

Finally the fulfilment of scripture links back to the opening bracket in 14:27 as the disciples flee, a flight which culminates in the burlesque of shameful desertion represented by the young man's naked flight (see p. 50). Pious tradition identifies the young man as Mark, the author of the gospel, perhaps on the grounds that he alone had the humility to mention it, while Matthew and Luke wanted to spare his blushes. To add to the confusion, the author of the gospel is then identified with John Mark, at whose family house the early community met (Acts 12:12). It is only surprising that the sheet (duly initialled) is, as yet, nowhere presented for veneration.

MATTHEW'S ACCOUNT – JESUS BETRAYED
Matthew 26:47–56

In many of the stories he shares with Mark, Matthew conveys an aura of solemnity and dignity about Jesus. In the healings of Simon's mother-in-law and the woman with a haemorrhage the crowds disappear and the sick woman stands reverently alone with Jesus. So in the arrest sequence Jesus is in complete control. The kernel is his response to Judas.[2] His address, 'Friend!', carries an invitation to repent, though also a reproach, for Matthew uses it twice elsewhere, on both occasions with an overtone of reproachful irony, to the labourer who grumbles at his wages and at the Master's generosity (20:13), and in the mouth of the King who asks the guest without a wedding garment for an explanation (22:12). In Matthew's writing it must also include an allusion to Ecclesiasticus (Sirach) 37:2, showing Jesus' awareness of the implications of Judas' actions, 'Is it not a deadly sorrow when a comrade or friend turns enemy?'

The enigmatic phrase which follows has eluded uncontroverted explanation: is it an exclamation, 'Friend, what you have come for!'? Is it a question, 'Friend, what have you come for?'? Is it elliptical,

---

[2] But there are other touches too: in 26:55 he addresses 'the crowds' in the plural, and reminds them that he was teaching 'seated' or 'enthroned' in the Temple, just as Moses was in giving the Law, or he himself for the Sermon on the Mount (5:1).

'Friend, *do* what you have come for'? In any case, it indicates Jesus' control of events. Only after this invitation can they arrest Jesus ('*then* they came forward' adds Matthew).

Matthew makes the assailant of the High Priest's servant 'one of those with Jesus', which enables him to lead on to three fearless teachings of Jesus, already captive. The first is typically Matthean in form (nicknamed by Goulder a 'machaeric'[3]), and may well be Matthew's application of the Wisdom saying in Genesis 9:6, 'He who sheds the blood of man, by man shall his blood be shed'. The second again shows Jesus' majestic and fearless response, as he refuses (in typically Matthean language and with typically Matthean hyperbole – 12 legions of angels should make 72,000) a supernatural aid from his Father. The third introduces the important teaching with which Matthew will conclude in 26:56: this moment is the fulfilment of the whole of scripture. This is the penultimate (the last being 27:9–10) and the most sweeping of the formula-quotations which stake out Matthew's gospel, showing that the whole of Jesus' life was centred on the fulfilment of scripture.

LUKE'S ACCOUNT – THE CAPTIVE HEALER
Luke 22:47–53

Luke simplifies the narrative, but also adds his own artistry. He has no interest in the arrangement of the sign, but increases the drama by its simplicity: first the crowd appears, then Judas detaches himself and goes straight up to Jesus to kiss him. Jesus knows that his kiss is the act of betrayal and challenges Judas – a challenge that stays hanging in the air. With his regard for picturesque material detail, Luke tells us that it was the right ear that was severed.[4]

---

[3] Goulder, 1974, p. 74 – a machaeric is Goulder's nickname for a four-point antithetical paradox, where two of the four terms are the same, as also Matthew 8:22; 10:40; 12:37, etc.

[4] This detail is also in John, raising the question as to whether there is a special link between Luke and John in the Passion Narrative, not shared by Mark and Matthew. In the course of the gospel there have been certain special similarities between Luke and John, e.g. the call of the disciples in Luke 5:1–11 and the appearance on the lake in John 21, the story of the centurion at Capernaum in Luke 7:1–10 and the royal official of Capernaum in John 4:46–53. In the Passion Narrative, however, the contacts become much more frequent and detailed: the

This gives the occasion for the first instance in which Jesus continues to exercise his healing ministry throughout the Passion, just as he will heal the enmity between Herod and Pilate, and as the whole Calvary scene is bathed in repentance. Jesus' concern to heal is an element which is stressed throughout Luke from the 'Nazareth Manifesto' onwards. There Jesus attests that his mission will be like that of Elisha who healed the Syrian Naaman (4:27). He does recount more physical healings than Mark, adding the healing of the widow's son (7:11–17) to that of Jairus' daughter (Mark 5:21–43/Luke 8:40–56), in his concern to pair women with men at every stage. However, the principal way in which Jesus' healing ministry comes to view is in the persistent stories of forgiveness (parables of the barren fig-tree, 13:6–9; the lost sheep, the lost coin and the prodigal son, 15:8–32). The Lukan Jesus does not wait for the sinner to admit sinfulness. He invites himself to Zacchaeus' feast when Zacchaeus has merely shown interest (19:3–5). The servant at the great banquet is instructed not to invite people (as Matthew 22:9), but to bring them in, even compel them to come in (14:21, 23). Luke's delicacy and concern is so great that he has been described as the *scriba mansuetudinis Christi*, 'the scribe of the gentleness of Jesus'. This comes to view in his finding excuses for the failing disciples: they lay down 'out of grief' (22:45); they failed to recognise him 'out of joy' (24:41). Perhaps the most perfect combination of both qualities is in the story of the woman who was a sinner (7:36–50): Jesus does not embarrass her by questioning her about repentance, but simply lets her pay her homage. While Matthew's indebted servant goes

---

anointing of Jesus' feet and the wiping by the woman's hair (Luke 7:38, 44 and John 12:3); the introduction of a discourse after the Last Supper (Luke 22:21–38 and John 14–17); amputation of the right ear (Luke 22:50 and John 18:10); the messianic challenge (Luke 22:66–67 'If you are the Christ, tell us' . . . 'If I tell you you do not believe' and John 10:24–25 'If you are the Christ, tell us' . . . 'I have told you and you do not believe'); Pilate's triple statement 'I find no cause in him' (Luke 23:4, 14, 22 and John 18:38; 19:4, 6); Mary and the return from the empty tomb (Luke 24:10 and John 20:9–10); Peter bends down and sees the burial-cloths (Luke 24:12 and John 20:5); the appearance in the upper room, especially Luke 24:26, 39, 40 and John 20:19, 20, 27); the Ascension (described by Luke 24:50–53 and mentioned by John 20:17). Whether there is direct contact between the two gospels or whether they both rely on the same oral source has been long disputed. There is also a vigorous argument that 'Luke knew and used John, and not vice versa' (Barbara Shellard, 1995, p. 98).

on his knees and begs for forgiveness (Matt. 18:26), in Luke's story Jesus offers forgiveness before it is asked. This offered forgiveness is the cause, not the result of love: 'which of them *therefore* will love him more?' (7:42). This touch of healing the servant's ear is just such a mark of tenderness as is typical of Luke.

Preparing also for Calvary, Luke omits any flight of the disciples, for Luke spares the disciples so that, instead of deserting, on Calvary 'all his friends stood at a distance' (23:49). On the other hand Luke draws the line with the stern warning to the chief priests, captains of the Temple and elders (who come themselves in Luke 22:52, not merely sending their minions). The time of freedom which began when Satan left Jesus after the testing in the desert (Luke 4:13) has come to an end.

On several small points there is an intriguing link to John. Firstly, the 'hour', which is so important in the expectation of the Passion in John, is mentioned. Only in Luke it is used in reverse, for the hour is that of his captors: 'This is your hour and the reign of darkness'. The symbolism of the darkness for the darkness of evil also rejoins that of John 13:30 ('As soon as Jesus had taken the piece of bread, he went out. It was night'). A third point is the presence of soldiers: John has the detachment of Roman soldiers, but Luke curiously includes in the arresting-party the 'generals' (literally) of the Temple. In Mark and Matthew the arrest is carried out by an ὄχλος, a crowd or even a rabble, a less disciplined body than in Luke and John.

JOHN'S ACCOUNT – 'I AM HE'
John 18:1–11

The awesome scene of the arrest dominates John's Passion Narrative. It sets the tone once and for all: Jesus is in total control, and himself exercises command, deciding what will happen and when it will happen. His captors merely follow his directions.

First we have the composition of place, which is in itself indicative and important. Mark and Matthew put the scene on the Mount of Olives, in a 'plot of land' called Gethsemane, a name which means merely 'olive-garden'. Luke omits the name, but it is characteristic of him to omit names which his gentile audience will find outlandish and strange. The important detail is that the name given by Mark and

Matthew scarcely adds to the general name 'Mount of Olives', and would hardly provide a precise location; their topography of Jerusalem is vague, raising doubts whether they knew the city at all. The whole hillside is, and no doubt was, covered with olive-orchards. By contrast John speaks immediately of crossing the Wadi[5] Kedron (18:1). Similarly in describing earlier visits of Jesus to Jerusalem the evangelist has moved easily around the city, referring to gates (the Sheep Gate) and pools (Bethzatha, Siloam), and to the nearby villages of Ephraim, Bethany and Bethphage – locations which can all be firmly established. He gives the impression of easy and flowing knowledge of Jerusalem, which makes the early twentieth-century assumption that the fourth gospel is factually totally unreliable all the more surprising.

THE KNOWLEDGE OF JESUS

After the briefest description of the arresting party, astoundingly Jesus comes out and takes the initiative. All the stress is on his knowledge and control of the situation. His uncanny knowledge of the unknowable and his foreknowledge have been features of the gospel. He sees and knows Nathanael under the fig-tree (1:48–50). He never needed evidence about anyone, for he could tell already (2:25). He knew from the outset who did not believe and who was to betray him (6:64). He knows that his 'hour' is not yet, and shows no fear of this moment (7:6). His knowledge amazed his opponents (7:14–17). He knows that his prayer to raise Lazarus to life will be answered (11:41–42). Especially from the beginning of the preliminaries to the Passion Narrative, Jesus' knowledge of what is to happened is underlined (13:1, 3). He knows in detail what Judas will do, and not merely does not stand in his way, but tells him positively, 'What you are to do, do quickly', with a certainty which suggests to the others that Judas is going on a specific errand (13:27). The whole of the Last Supper narrative is heavy with foreboding, set off by Jesus washing the feet of the disciples as

---

[5] The Greek word means 'stream which flows in winter', which is exactly the meaning of 'Wadi'. Many of the stream-beds east of Jerusalem are dry all summer, and flow, sometimes only for a few hours, after the winter rains. This is the case with the Kedron – or presumably was, before it was converted into being the chief sewer of East Jerusalem.

an acted parable of the act of service which is to come, and extended into the mysterious talk of going away and returning (14:28–30; 16:5, 16, etc). This foreknowledge of Jesus is presented by John so uncompromisingly that on its own it poses a serious difficulty for understanding the balance with Jesus' human acquisition of knowledge. It must be weighed against such statements as Luke 2:52, 'Jesus increased in wisdom, in stature and in favour with God and with people'.

THE SELF-PRESENTATION OF THE JOHANNINE JESUS

In the synoptic gospels Jesus concentrates on presenting and bringing to reality the renewal of the reign of God. In John the kingdom of God has receded into the background and Jesus concentrates on presenting himself, particularly in his relationship to his Father. It is arguable that there are in John two layers of Christology, one a prophetic Christology, in which Jesus claims to be a second Moses (especially in John 6:31–58). This identification is a messianic claim, not passing beyond bounds which were acceptable within Judaism, for others had claimed to be Messiah, reinforced by claims to repeat the miracles of Moses. There is, however, also a second layer in the Johannine Jesus' teaching about himself which was utterly unacceptable to 'the Jews'. One of the most expressive ways in which this is presented occurs in 5:19–30. It is the prerogative of God to work on the Sabbath, giving life (because babies are born on the Sabbath) and exercising judgement (because people die on the Sabbath). After Jesus has cured the sick man at the Pool of Bethzatha on the Sabbath, in answer to the Jewish objections he explains that both these powers are given to the Son, so that the Son is seen to share the position and prerogatives of the Father. This is a sort of dynamic, rather than static, definition of equality, for if the Father and the Son share the same powers this is a Hebrew way of saying they share the same nature:

> The hour is coming – indeed it is already here – when the dead will hear the voice of the Son of God, and all who hear it will live. For as the Father has life in himself, so he has granted the Son also to have life in himself.
>
> And because he is the Son of man he has granted him power

to give judgement. For the hour is coming when the dead will leave their graves at the sound of his voice (5:25–28).

The most expressive way of all, however, is in Jesus' use of the phrase 'I am' (ἐγώ εἰμι). Like many of John's phrases ('living water', 'born again') this is in itself ambiguous, and can be understood in several ways. At one level it is simply a self-identification, as in answering the door, 'Yes, it's me.' This is the level at which it should probably be understood in the synoptic gospels, e.g. when Jesus appears walking on the water and calms the fears of the disciples that they are seeing an apparition by identifying himself, 'Courage! It's me! Don't be afraid!' (Mark 6:50). At a deeper level the Johannine Jesus uses it as a means to claim for himself ways in which God had always been understood in the Bible: 'I am the light of the world (8:12, compare Wisd. 7:26) . . . the good shepherd (10:7–18, compare Ezekiel 34) . . . the resurrection (11:25) . . . the way, the truth and life' (14:6, compare Psalm 36:9). At a still deeper level it is used absolutely and without predicate with allusion to the unpronounceable Name of God. In Exodus 3:14 God revealed his Name to Moses as 'Yahweh'. With the widespread Hebrew love of giving a meaning to names,[6] this was explained as meaning 'I am who I am'. By the time of Jesus this was understood, at any rate in hellenistic Judaism (and John was not written in narrowly Palestinian circles), as meaning ὁ ὢν, 'He who Is', perhaps best rendered philosophically as 'absolute Being'. There is also allusion to the frequent use of this expression to designate God in Deutero-Isaiah, especially in polemical passages against idolatry and polytheism, e.g. Isaiah 43:10–11, 'No god was formed before me, nor will be after me. I am, I am Yahweh'.

The great round of controversies between Jesus and 'the Jews' in the Temple centres on Jesus' claim to this title. Owing to the ambiguity of the expression, the first two uses can, at a pinch, be understood as mere self-identifications. About the third there is no such ambiguity, for it makes sense no other way than as a divine claim, and it is at the third usage that they react to blasphemy by picking up stones to throw at him:

---

[6] E.g. Gen. 29:32–35; 1 Sam. 4:21–22.

If you do not believe that I am He (ἐγώ εἰμι), you will die in your sins (John 8:24).

When you have lifted up the Son of man, then you will know that I am He, (ἐγώ εἰμι) (8:28).

In all truth I tell you, before Abraham ever was, I am, (ἐγώ εἰμι) (8:58).

Now in the garden Jesus takes the initiative to use the title. Instead of Judas starting off the process by his greeting, Jesus asks the first question. It is the question asked throughout the gospel of all who seek Jesus, first to the disciples in the Jordan Valley, 'What do you seek?' (1:38) and finally to Mary Magdalene, 'Whom do you seek?' (20:15). To their reply Jesus answers with ἐγώ εἰμι. At one level it is a mere self-identification, but, typically of John, its real meaning is shown by the reaction of the arresting party, who retreat and fall to the ground, the stock reaction to a divine vision (Dan. 2:46; Rev. 1:17). The ἐγώ εἰμι is thus repeated three times (18:5, 6, 8) for emphasis.

The same emphasis on Jesus' control of the scene continues in the final two elements of the arrest. Jesus commands on the authority of scripture that the disciples should be allowed to go free (18:8–9). Finally he commands Peter to sheath his sword, not for any reason of morality, but for a Christocentric reason, lest Peter should interfere with the Father's will for the Son to drink the cup (18:11).

5

BEFORE THE HIGH PRIEST

The first question to be faced with regard to this gospel scene is its historical intention. Is Mark relating what he knows to have happened from historical information, or is he deducing what must have happened, relying on a Christian view of the condemnation and death of Jesus? The former alternative is the traditional Christian position. It is normally undergirded with the assertion that, unlike the agony and the arrest, this was an inherently public scene, to which there would have been many witnesses. Mark, as the trusted representative of the Christian community, could not simply have spun this story from his perspective of faith. He would never have got away with it. He would have been howled down if he had invented things. Anyway, it bears the stamp of eye-witness detail. Nevertheless, the position that Mark is relying exclusively on detailed historical information brings with it certain difficulties:

'The stamp of eye-witness detail' simply means that the story is well told. It must be conceded from the outset that Mark is a brilliant story-teller, which was no doubt part of the reason why he was chosen to put down the first record of the Good News to have survived.

The contention that a story not based on historical knowledge, and not corresponding more or less exactly to known facts, could not have survived the criticism of the Christian community presupposes a modern view of historical writing. If both Mark and his audience shared a different perspective on how history should be written, a record of the message of Jesus less mechanically consonant with known facts could well have been the most acceptable. As we have seen, (pp. 17–27) comparison between the gospel writers leaves no doubt that they felt justified in massaging and even changing known historical details to express their theology more clearly. Comparison with other contemporary writers – historical writers, let alone those concerned to present a particular message – leaves no doubt that it was felt legitimate for historians to use a good deal of latitude, e.g. in the composition of speeches. Josephus often gives considerably different versions of an event in his two works, *The Jewish War* and *The Antiquities of the Jews*. Luke's three versions of the vocation of Paul within the same work (the Acts of the Apostles) show significant variations.

The gospel of John contains no record of an appearance before the High Priest and the sanhedrin after Jesus' arrest. He mentions considerably earlier a meeting of the High Priest, Caiaphas, with his advisors at which the decision is taken to do away with Jesus (11:47–53). After Jesus' arrest there is only an appearance (18:19–24) before Annas, the former High Priest, which has some similarities with the Mark/Matthew account, especially in the details about Peter's denials.

The two judicial appearances, before the High Priest and before Pilate, are so similar in structure that they appear to have been modelled on each other, or at least composed by the same hand (see pp. 84–86).

Though Mark and Matthew relate what is basically the same event, the differences in Luke's account could almost suggest that he is narrating a different event. The most striking difference is that the High Priest is absent from his story (see p. 78). Mark's account is so imbued with his own language and narrative techniques that it is hard to see that he could have been relying on any written source. At most, he is putting an orally received narrative into his own words. Among the narrative techniques may be mentioned Mark's technique of intercalation or 'sandwiching' (see chapter 1, note 23) and his triple repetition (see chapter 1, note 25). As in the triple repetition during the agony, he seems to have enough material for one account (14:66–68 give a lively account in his best eye-witness style), while the second and third are somewhat flat. As for language, Mark's own Greek text is replete with his characteristic style.[1]

---

[1] E.g. double negative (14:60, 61); double statement (14:61 and 68 and 71); double location ('inside . . . into the hall', 14:54; ἐξῆλθεν ἔξω 14:68); double question (14:63 and 64, cf. Neirynck, 1988); impersonal plural (14:53); periphrastic

MARK'S ACCOUNT
Mark 14:53–72

The account has three centres of interest, the false accusations about the Temple, the Christological declaration and Peter's triple denial.

The threat to destroy the Temple and in three days to rebuild it occurs in some form or other in the gospel with important frequency; it must have been a feature of Jesus' teaching. It provides the context for the teaching about the future of Jesus' community which he gives over-looking the Temple (Mark 13:2), when he says that not one of those magnificent stones will be left upon another. The threat is symbolically fulfilled by Jesus' demonstration in the Temple itself, which Mark portrays (through framing it by the story of the cursing of the barren fig-tree, 11:12–21) as a declaration of the sterility of Israel. It is picked up by the mockers at the crucifixion (15:29). Its importance is reinforced by its occurrence in a quite different context in John 2:19.

The interest of this saying is that the renewal of the Temple was an important part of the current eschatological expectation of the messianic renewal, attested in Jewish literature of all kinds.[2] An early witness comes in the Book of Henoch 90:28–29 (a section dated to the early second century BC):

> I went on looking till the Lord of the sheep brought about a new house, greater and loftier than the first one, and set it up in the first location which had been covered up. All its pillars were new, the columns new and the ornaments new as well as greater than those of the first, the old house which was gone. All the sheep were within it.

At the other extreme, in the first century AD, possibly after the destruction of the Temple, two Palestinian Targums attest the same hope:

---

imperfect (14:54); ὅτι-recitative (14:58, 69, 72); the ubiquitous πάλιν (14:61 and 70 twice); asyndeton (14:64); ἤρξαντο with infinitives (14:65 and 69 and 71); numerals (14:58 and 72, cf. Elliott, 1993, p. 61); καὶ εὐθὺς (14:72). How typical these are of Mark may be seen by the frequency with which Matthew and Luke avoid them: of these 24 little instances of Markan style in this passage Matthew retains only 7 and Luke (though of course his text is fairly different) none.

[2] See Isa. 14:5; 54:1; Tob. 13:16–17; Jub. 1:15–17; Ps-Sal. 17:32; 1 QM 7:4–10; 4Q Flor 1:6–7; 4 QpPs. 37 3:11; 11 QTemple 29:8–10; Rev. 21:22.

He will build the temple which was profaned because of our
transgressions and delivered up because of our sins (Tg Isa. 53:5).

The Messiah will be revealed and will be exalted and he will build
the temple of the Lord[3] (Tg Zech. 6:12).

The same hope is strongly attested at Qumran, a quite different section
of the contemporary tradition, e.g.

For behold a son is born to Jesse. [He is to take] the Rock of Zion
and build a house for the Lord, the God of Israel (4Q522).

Or 4Q174, commenting on 2 Sam 7:10:

This is the house which [he will build for them] in the last
days ... This is the house into which [the unclean shall] never
enter ... [Its glory shall endure] for ever; it shall appear above it
perpetually.

In the main Rule of the Community (1 QS 8:5–9) it is, as in 1 Cor.
3:16, the community which forms the Temple:

The Council of the Community shall be established in truth. It
shall be that tried wall, that precious cornerstone, whose foun-
dations shall neither rock nor sway in their place. It shall be a
most holy dwelling for Aaron, with everlasting knowledge of the
covenant of justice, and shall offer up sweet fragrance.

The renewal of the Temple is, then, a part of Jesus' messianic claim
which would strike an immediate chord with his contemporaries.

There is a strong case to be made that it was this attitude towards
the Temple, put into practice by Jesus symbolically rubbishing the
Temple, which led to his arrest through the determination of the Temple
authorities to get rid of him. On the one hand his consistent, or rather
persistent, re-interpretation of the Law on such matters as Sabbath
observance (Mark 2:23–28; 3:1–6), purity (7:14–23) and divorce
(10:1–12) would no doubt have infuriated the Pharisees. But it does
not go beyond the bounds of tolerable disagreement between rabbinic
schools. His exorcisms were explained away as the product of a pact

[3] Cathcart, 1989.

with Beelzebul (3:22). His cures were not all that much materially different from those credited to other charismatic Galilean rabbis[4] – except that he saw them as signs that the reign of God was breaking out (Matt. 11:2–15). His forgiveness of sin on his own authority (Mark 2:5–10), short-circuiting the accepted methods of purification, was a further sign of his disregard of accepted conventions and a proclamation of a 'brokerless kingdom of God'. Even all these put together do not seem to have provoked any decisive move against Jesus. However, when he upsets the business of the Temple, the Temple authorities take action. Especially at the Passover, for which Josephus claims one-and-a-half million pilgrims came to Jerusalem, such a disturbance cannot be risked again.

Significantly, it is the Temple authorities, the chief priests, who take the lead in all the action against Jesus. The Pharisees disappear from the scene after Mark 12:13, and take no part in the Passion. In Matthew similarly they take no part in the Passion, though they reappear in Matthew 27:62 to ensure a guard at the tomb. In Mark the scribes (lawyers, the official interpreters of the Law) continue to appear occasionally, namely for the original plot in 14:1, for the arrest in 14:43, at the trial in 14:53 and 15:1, and for the mockery of Jesus on the cross in 15:31. Matthew, however, writing for an audience to whom functions within Judaism were better known, is more careful, and cuts them out on all these occasions except the last. They are mere interpreters of the Law, not men of action. This leaves the concentration of the action in the hands of the chief priests and elders. Such concentration coheres with the view that it was Jesus' action against the Temple that brought him to grief.

Why then does Mark attribute the pivotal saying about the Temple to false witnesses, when it is well-attested as Jesus' own, and important for understanding the course of events? Most likely it is put in the mouths of false witnesses to show the fulfilment of prophecy. It is a scriptural allusion to the false witnesses standing up against the Just Man, as in the psalms:

---

[4] The stories of the miracles of Rabbi Honi the Circle-Drawer and Rabbi Hanina ben Dosa may be found in G. Vermes, 1973, pp. 69–77.

> False witnesses have risen against me, and are breathing out
> violence (Ps. 27:12). False witnesses come forward against me,
> asking me questions I cannot answer (Ps. 35:11).

Jesus' lack of response is also a scriptural allusion. His silence echoes
that of the Suffering Servant of Yahweh:

> Ill-treated and afflicted,
>   he never opened his mouth.
> Like a lamb led to the slaughter-house,
>   like a sheep dumb before its shearers,
>   he never opened his mouth (Isa. 53:7).

This theme will recur in the trial before Pilate and before Herod (15:4;
Luke 23:9).

The two charges from false witnesses, then, provide no evidence.
But the statement about renewal of the Temple, conventionally a task
for the Messiah, leads directly to the High Priest's question, challenging
Jesus to acknowledge his Messiahship. It is important that no progress
can be made except by Jesus' own statement. The third question, this
time by the High Priest himself, evokes the full declaration of the
personality of Jesus. Hitherto in Mark Jesus has sought to conceal his
identity by a process which has often been called 'the Messianic Secret'.
He has forbidden those whom he healed to reveal his identity (1:44;
7:36). He has commanded the unclean spirits who proclaim him as
'son of God' to be silent (1:25; 3:12). He has forbidden his disciples
to proclaim the message of the Transfiguration 'until the son of man
had risen from the dead' (Mark 9:9). The first half of the gospel has
shown the long, halting process of instruction which finally issues in
Peter's declaration at Caesarea Philippi that Jesus is the Christ, the
Messiah (8:29). Even then Peter is silenced, and the further process
begins, equally halting, of teaching the disciples what sort of Messiah
he is, one who must suffer and be rejected. Three times Jesus prophesies
the Passion and rejection; each time the disciples miss the point, and
each time he must reiterate that his followers must share with him the
way of suffering and humiliation (8:31–38; 9:31–37; 10:32–45). Not
until Jesus has died on the cross does any human being acknowledge
that he is son of God (15:39). But for the audience of the gospel the

full revelation of his identity comes already at the interrogation by the High Priest. This is the bursting of the messianic secret.

The High Priest's question focuses on two titles, 'Messiah' and 'son of the Blessed One'. To these Jesus adds a third, the mysterious self-identification, 'son of man'. The expression 'son of God' is used in the Bible in several ways, and the discovery of what it means when used of Jesus has been the process of Mark's gospel. It can be used of angels (Job 1:9), of Israel (Hosea 11:1), of leaders of the people (Ps. 82:6), and even of the just (Wisd. 2:18). Of itself, then, it denotes a special relationship with God, but in ways still to be defined by the context. The introduction to the gospel has shown the audience of the gospel that Jesus is son of God by the heading, 'The beginning of the gospel of Jesus Christ, son of God'[5] (1:1) and the Voice at the Baptism (1:11), renewed at the Transfiguration (9:7). The spirits expelled by Jesus have reiterated the title (1:24; 5:7). Now it receives its fullest explanation by means of Jesus' reply. This combines two texts, Psalm 110:1 and Daniel 7:13, in the manner common not only in Christian usage but already in the Qumran commentaries on scripture or *pesharim*.[6] The former of these is the text most frequently of all used in the New Testament of the Risen Christ (Rom. 8:34; 1 Cor. 15:25; Eph. 1:20; Col. 3:1; Heb. 1:3; 8:1; 10:12–13; 12:2). The latter attributes to Jesus the role given by Daniel to the representative of Israel to whom God gives all power and authority. Mark has already used this text in 8:38 and 13:26 of the coming of Jesus on the Day of the Lord. Together the two texts constitute a Markan assertion, at this moment of seeming judgement, of the ultimate triumph of Jesus.

The reaction of the High Priest in accusing Jesus of blasphemy has been variously interpreted. One difficulty has been to see how Jesus' reply is technically blasphemous. Later rabbinic rules demand that blasphemy should include the name of God, but we have no knowledge of such technicalities at the time of Jesus. Nor was it blasphemous to claim to be the Messiah. However, the Greek word βλασφημέω is considerably wider than 'blaspheme', and can include other arrogant and insulting behaviour. It must also be remembered that we are moving

---

[5] This text is uncertain, the words 'son of God' being omitted in some important manuscripts.
[6] This is fully argued and explained by Perrin, 1967, pp. 173–185.

on the Markan rather than the historical level.[7] Two assertions are being made, the first about the position of Jesus, the second about the reaction to it by the High Priest. The first assertion, made by means of the scriptural allusions, amounts to putting Jesus on a level with God, seated at the right hand of God on the divine throne, and coming with the clouds at the Day of the Lord. A further dimension is suggested by the clash between 'seated' and 'coming': if the two are meant to be simultaneous, the only way in which Jesus can be both seated and coming is if he shares the chariot-throne of God described in Ezekiel 1. In later Jewish mysticism the chariot-throne in this vision of Ezekiel became an important focus; but it is already a significant centre of devotion at Qumran (4Q405). If the combination of the two texts is meant deliberately to suggest such an allusion, the blasphemy is indeed horrific. The second assertion, in the reaction of the High Priest to what he and his councillors take to be intolerable arrogance, amounts in fact to a statement that Jesus' claims were the ultimate reason for his rejection and condemnation.

The mockery which concludes the interchange between Jesus and the High Priest and his council is a fulfilment of the Song of the Servant in Isaiah 50:6,

> I have offered my back to those who struck me,
> my cheeks to those who plucked my beard.
> I have not turned my face away from insult and spitting.

The humiliation of the spitting and mockery is an unpleasantly suitable response to the accusation of arrogance implied by the High Priest's charge of βλασφημία. It is also a typical instance of Mark's irony that they should mock Jesus for the prophecy which Mark's readers know to be true. It is made more ironical by occurring just when Jesus' prophecy about Peter's betrayal is at the point of fulfilment.

Peter's triple denial brings to a climax the theme of the inadequacy and failure of the disciples which has been such an important element

---

[7] Similarly Brown, 1994, p. 482, wisely insists (with italics): 'the high priest's question was *not* the formulation in a Jewish investigation of Jesus in AD 30/33', on the grounds that the title 'son of God' was not applied to Jesus during his lifetime.

in Mark's gospel. The scene is brilliantly expressed by Mark. It is easy to imagine Peter penetrating right into the courtyard (ἕως ἔσω), lost in the crowd of retainers (συγκαθήμενος) and warming himself at the fire, and then slipping out after the first challenge. Inherent in the positioning is the contrast between Jesus' steadfastness and Peter's cowardice. There is also a strong contrast between the sturdy Peter and the servant-girl. The word παιδίσκη is a diminutive and may suggest 'a slip of a girl'; the same word is used of the idiotic servant-girl in Acts 12:13 who shuts out Peter after his miraculous release from prison. As in the case of the triple prayer in Gethsemane, there is some suggestion that Mark himself tripled the denial, for the flatness of the second denial contrasts with the liveliness of the first, suggesting that Mark lacked material. Traces of the break would remain in Peter's exit at 14:69, which also makes the next denial awkward. But the third denial is lively enough.

MATTHEW'S ACCOUNT
Matthew 26:57–75

Matthew does a good deal towards tightening up Mark's account. Stylishly he brackets the scene neatly through Peter going 'in inside' (εἰσελθὼν ἔσω) at the beginning and coming 'out outside' (ἐξελθὼν ἔξω) at the end. The change to the long drawn out imperfect tense (ἠκολούθει, 'he was following, he kept following') from the snappy aorist in 26:58 may also be intended to indicate Peter's hesitant and stealthy approach.

Theologically more important, however, is the decisive build-up in three successive 'shots'. First they deliberately seek false witness in order to put him to death; this neatly exploits Mark's accent on false witnesses not because of their falsity but – in reliance on the psalms – because of their hostility.

Then a sharp distinction is made by the Matthean 'but afterwards' and the *two* witnesses, firmly indicating the validity of their witness to Jesus' saying, and making Mark's 14:59 ('But even on this point their evidence was conflicting') inappropriate. The saying itself is simplified and altered too, no longer indicating that Jesus *will* destroy the Temple, but that he *could*. It is a statement of his messianic power, a power greater than the Temple (cf. Matt. 12:6).

This leads on to a noble and dramatic build-up to Jesus' crucial declaration: the High Priest rises to his feet, is twice confronted with Jesus' silence and then elicits full solemnity by putting Jesus under oath by the living God – an awesome biblical challenge (cf. Gen. 24:3; Judg. 21:7). At the same time the High Priest is unaware that he is ironically echoing Peter's confession in 16:16, 'You are the Christ, the son of the living God'. The dramatic confrontation is increased by diverse touches: 'Tell us!', says the High Priest insistently. 'You said it yourself', retorts Jesus emphatically, 'and what's more, from this moment on . . . ' Jesus accepts the titles offered by the High Priest but amplifies them in his own sense (πλὴν, 'except', suggests an adversative correction), stressing also his own knowledge and control, as at the very beginning of the Passion sequence (26:2). The strength of the confrontation continues with the immediacy of the Matthean 'then' (τότε) and the High Priest's explosive, 'He has blasphemed!' In Mark 14:63 the High Priest merely asks the question; in Matthew he begins by giving the answer, and reiterates, '*Look now!* You have heard the blasphemy.' It is an angry and forceful scene, mercilessly rounded off by three further touches in the mockery: the mockers are no longer anonymous 'certain people' (τινες) as in Mark, but 'they', who can only be the councillors. Secondly, Mark's blindfolding veil (14:65) is removed, lest it should protect Jesus from the spitting. Thirdly, the messianic point of the whole scene is once again stressed by the mockers' gibe, '*Christ*, who is it that struck you?'

The same merciless dramatic intensity sharpens Matthew's account of Peter's denials. The three mark a crescendo of harassment, each by different challengers as poor Peter moves vainly around to escape attention. First Matthew increases the intimacy by introducing the name of Jesus in 26:69. Despite this, Peter denies 'before all' (ἔμπροσθεν πάντων), the public denial surely contrasting with the demand in Matthew 10:33 for the disciple to confess Jesus before all (ἔμπροσθεν τῶν ἀνθρώπων). On the second occasion Peter denies 'with an oath' – in the teeth of Jesus' prohibition of oaths in the Sermon on the Mount (5:34). It is not surprising that on the third occasion Peter runs out and 'wept *bitterly*' (26:75). The scene is made all the more tragic by being the last appearance of Peter in the gospel. In Mark there was at any rate the implication of forgiveness in the message at the empty tomb, 'Go and tell his disciples and Peter' (Mark 16:7); in Matthew there is no hint of reconciliation. Just as Peter's bold attempt to join Jesus walking on the waters (Matthew 14:30) made him the apostle of failed good intentions, so now his bold attempt to stay with Jesus in his trials makes him the first publicly to deny his Master.

LUKE'S ACCOUNT – PREPARATION OF CHARGES
Luke 22:54–71

The account of the night's activities given by Luke is importantly different from those of Mark and Matthew. Most obviously, the timing and order of events is different. It may well be more correct, for a nocturnal meeting of the High Priest and his council is not likely, especially on the eve of the Passover Feast. Was Mark (followed by Matthew) drawn into this timing by the tradition expressed in 1 Cor. 11:23, 'On the night he was betrayed . . .'? Luke will have known that Roman magistrates held their levée early in the morning (Verres, the notorious governor of Sicily prosecuted by Cicero, held his in bed!). He treats the whole judicial proceedings as one process, regarding the Jewish element as a mere preparation of charges.[8] There is nothing approaching a verdict or decision; it merely ends when they feel that they have enough evidence, whereupon they all spring up and take Jesus off to Pilate. This is the same sort of timing as occurs in the Acts of the Apostles, when the apostles are interrogated by the rulers, elders and scribes after a night in custody (Acts 4:5, cf. 5:21; 22:30); it was no doubt normal throughout the Roman world.[9] Luke obviously sensibly considers also that it makes more sense to fill the night with Peter's denials, when the warming fire is suitable, and – as time goes on – the crowing cock. There Luke's particular contribution is to show the Lord turning towards Peter and provoking his repentance (22:61). There is still time in the morning for a brief mockery of Jesus by his guards.

When the meeting (on the translation of the Greek word *sanhedrin* here, see above, pp. 35–36) is eventually held the procedure is again different. The elders of the people, the chief priests and the scribes are

---

[8] 'A formal condemnation by the *presbyterion* would destroy the dramatic effect of Luke's composition', says Matera, 1989, p. 532.

[9] This is still normal practice in Jerusalem. Noisy queues are forming from 4 a.m. outside the Palestinian Permits Office opposite my window as I write.

present (Luke seems to feel that these last should be present as lawyers
in preparing the charges), but there is no mention of the High Priest
himself anywhere in the proceedings. Consequently the proceedings
have been qualified as 'a kangaroo court' and the participants likened
to leaderless children, ganging up on their victim. However, as a preparation of charges it makes good sense, and perhaps Luke thought it
beneath the High Priest's grandeur.

The content of the proceedings has also been fine-tuned. For Luke
the Temple was and remained an important element. The 'cleansing
of the Temple' is properly so called for him; there is no violence, no
explanation of the barrenness of Israel through the bracketing by the
withered fig-tree, simply an expulsion of the dealers, so that it may be
once more a house of prayer (19:45–46). Indeed it becomes the focus
of Jesus' activity in Jerusalem as he teaches daily in the Temple (19:47).
It will remain the focus of the life of the ideal Jerusalem community
after the Resurrection (Acts 2:46; 3:1–11; 5:12, 20–21), until Stephen's
speech registers the refusal of mainstream Judaism to take its opportunity. Hence there is no mention of destruction of the Temple among
the charges, nor later in the mockery of Jesus on the cross. Instead two
separate questions are put to Jesus, divided by that curiously Johannine
statement of Jesus[10] of their refusal to accept his testimony. The High
Priest's single composite question in Mark is divided into two, firstly
'Are you the Christ?' and secondly 'Are you the son of God?'. These
are the two closely related titles of Jesus which Luke has already linked
in the message of the angel at the Annunciation (1:32, 'Son of the
Most High' and 'son of David') and in the mouths of expelled demons
(4:41). These are the two questions put to Jesus in the Johannine
controversy in the Temple, first challenging Jesus in much the same
words as used here (John 10:24–25, see p. 82) to tell them if he is the
Christ, the second reproaching him for blasphemy for the claim to be
Son of God (John 10:36). They are the two most common titles of
Jesus in the Pauline writings, reflecting the emphases of the earliest
community. In Jesus' answer to the former question Luke concentrates
on the position of Jesus, seated at the right hand of God. That is his
position, where he is ready to receive Christians, withdrawing any

---

[10] Cf. John 10:24–25. On possible links between John and Luke, see chapter 4,
note 4.

attention from an eschatological coming on the clouds. Jesus is here his own witness, and when his first martyr-witness faces the members of the sanhedrin, Stephen sees the Son of man standing ready to receive him (Acts 7:56). The second question receives the greater emphasis: they 'all' ask it, in chorus, and the answer sends them hurrying off to Pilate. There is no doubt in Luke that the reason for the rejection of Jesus was his claim to be Son of God.

JOHN'S ACCOUNT: CONDEMNATION BY CAIAPHAS, CONFRONTATION WITH ANNAS
John 11:45–54; 18:12–27

Of all the material differences between John and the synoptics, the disparity over the investigation/trial by Caiaphas is at first sight the most intractable (with the possible exception of the call of the first disciples). The chronology of the synoptic gospels stems by and large from Mark, and Mark puts Jesus' only contact with and visit to Jerusalem in the final week of his life. Fascinated with numbers, Mark even notes down the days ('next day', 11:12; 'next morning', 11:20; 'it was two days before the Passover', 14:1; 'on the first day of Unleavened Bread, 14:12), just as he will note the hours of Jesus' last day (15:25, 33, 34, 42). The limitation of Jesus' presence in Jerusalem to this last week would seem to exclude any possibility of the Lazarus incident and its sequels which lead up to the decision by Caiaphas and his company to liquidate Jesus (John 11:45–53). Only when this Markan final week is seen as one more instance of Mark's selection and grouping of events is the way left open for acceptance of the Lazarus-sequence. Among the most obvious groups of events whose organisation may be attributed to Mark are 2:1–3:6, controversies with the Pharisees in Galilee; 4:1–34, parables; 12:13–37, final controversies with Jerusalem authorities. Nor can it pass unnoticed that the waving of branches and the singing of Psalm 118 at the solemn entry into Jerusalem fit the Feast of Sukkoth in the autumn much more appropriately than the casual moment of pilgrims arriving a few days before Passover.

Once the tyranny of Markan chronology has been set aside, the way is open to accepting a three-stage process leading up to the trial by Pilate, namely:

1. Decision by Caiaphas, chief priests (and Pharisees?) to liquidate
   Jesus (11:46–53)
2. Arrangements with Roman authorities to provide armed assistance
   at the arrest
3. Investigation by Annas (18:12–14, 19–24).

1. The decision to kill Jesus in John 11:46–53 does not necessarily
   clash with the synoptic scene of the investigation of Jesus by Caiaphas. It could well be a preliminary decision made, as its position
   in John suggests, some time before the arrest. It is a supreme
   example of Johannine irony, Caiaphas unknowingly acknowledging
   Jesus' power to save the people and the scattered children of God.
   Josephus cites other instances of prophecy by the High Priest (*War*,
   1.68; *Antiquities*, 11.327; 13.299). At the same time on another level
   Caiaphas is wrong, for their action did not prevent the Romans
   coming and suppressing the Temple. There is even more irony, and
   typical Johannine duality, in the fact that Jesus' gift of life to Lazarus
   leads to his own death.

   This is one of the isolated passages where the Pharisees take an
   active role in proceedings towards the death of Jesus, as they also
   do in the Johannine scene of the arrest (18:3). It is, however, notable
   that in the reference back to both these scenes given in 18:12–14
   those involved are described simply as 'the Jews'. A strong case is
   made by Urban von Wahlde, 'there can be no doubt that these two
   sets of terms for religious authorities stem from different authors'.[11]
   The earlier terminology, by which the opposition to Jesus comes
   from the Pharisees, dates from a time when there was still memory
   of the actual groups within Judaism (Pharisees, Sadducees, scribes)
   and of 'family feuding' within Judaism between followers of Jesus
   and those who would not accept him (the Pharisees), whereas later
   the memory of these distinctions has become blurred, and opposition
   is simply from 'the Jews'. This produces the strange situation that
   those who are in fact Jews can be said to be 'afraid of the Jews'
   (John 7:13; 9:22; 20:19). Attempts have been made to relieve John
   of apparent anti-Semitism by interpreting these passages as referring

---

[11] von Wahlde, 1989, p. 35.

to the inhabitants of Judaea. In fact, however, only a limited number of passages can be realistically so interpreted (e.g. 11:8, 33, 45, 54). It is more honest and realistic to accept that John's harsh statements express the reaction to expulsion from the synagogue as a result of a high Christology (9:22), and the bitter controversy which followed from that.[12]

2. Only in the Johannine account does the arresting party include Roman auxiliary troops 'together with guards sent by the chief priests and the Pharisees' (18:3), the troop or σπεῖρα being commanded by a tribune (18:12). Normally a σπεῖρα would indicate a cohort of 600. That it was a sizeable number, even if not a full cohort, is indicated also by the description of the commander as a χιλίαρχος (literally 'commander of 1,000'). The size of the detachment may be read as an indication of the power and dignity of Jesus whom they are to arrest. More important, however, is the very presence of Roman troops, which indicates that by this time the Jewish authorities have convinced the Romans that Jesus poses at least a *prima facie* threat. This links in with the absence in John of any attempt by a Jewish tribunal to prepare charges against Jesus.

3. The appearance before Annas has a quite different quality to the synoptic appearance before Caiaphas and his council. Not only are the personalities different. Annas, though called the High Priest (18:19), was no longer in office. He had been High Priest for nine years till deposed in AD 15, but he retained a uniquely powerful position (Josephus, *Antiquities*, 20.198) as father of five and father-in-law of one High Priest, the current incumbent Caiaphas (High Priest AD 18–36). Furthermore, the meeting is a solemn one-to-one confrontation, apart from the intrusion in one verse of a guard. Most

---

[12] Until recently it was current to associate this virulent anti-Judaism with the split occurring after the Synod of Jamnia (or Yavneh), and the introduction there of the Twelfth of the Eighteen Benedictions, which contained the Curse on the Heretics and the Christians (*minim* and *nozrim*). Although it seems accepted that Vespasian gave the rabbis leave to gather at Jamnia and so begin the repair of Judaism after the Fall of Jerusalem, it is now much more doubtful that any single, datable Synod took place. It is also doubtful whether the Twelfth 'Benediction' existed in anything like its present form until the end of the second century cf. van der Horst, 1994. There is therefore no clear date for the beginning of virulent hostility between Synagogue and Church. It is best dated imprecisely 'in the closing years of the first century'.

notable of all, it can hardly be called an interrogation by Annas. There is no suggestion of any accusation, charge or condemnation. Indeed, any judgement of Jesus by the Jews is precluded theologically, for, as we shall see, Jesus judges the Jews, not *vice versa*. There is no need for Jesus to explain his position or his identity, for he has already done so in the Temple, and with words reminiscent of the interrogation scene in the synoptics, especially Luke:

> 'If you are the Christ, tell us' . . . He replied, 'If I tell you . . . you will not believe' (Luke 22:67).
> 'If you are the Christ, tell us openly.' Jesus replied, 'I have told you, but you do not believe' (John 10:24–25).

True, the confrontation begins with Annas addressing a question to Jesus, but Jesus is in control of the whole scene and continues the teaching which he has done in the Temple. The High Priest is a passive dummy: while the statements of Jesus are explicit, the High Priest's words are never quoted. Jesus reproaches his captors just as he reproached his stubborn listeners in the Temple. He is seen, as throughout John's gospel, as the public teacher of Israel, the embodiment of divine Wisdom. 'I have spoken openly for all the world to hear' (18:20) both sums up Jesus' teaching in the Temple in John 7–8 and alludes to the great judgement scene in Isaiah, when Yahweh, the Creator of the world, declares:

> I am Yahweh and there is no other,
> I have not spoken in secret, in some dark corner of the underworld,
> I am Yahweh, I proclaim saving justice. I say what is true.
>   (Isaiah 45:18–19)

In accordance with this divine status, the mockery by the attendants in the synoptic gospels is reduced to one blow by a guard to which Jesus has the final word with a dignified riposte. This too is reminiscent of Jesus' teaching in the Temple,

> 'Can any of you convict me of sin? If I speak the truth, why do you not believe me?' (8:46)
> 'If there is some offence in what I said, point it out; but if not, why do you strike me?' (18:23)

After the full and explicit Johannine teaching of Jesus in the Temple there is no need for a scene of interrogation by the Jewish authorities to explain how and why Jesus was handed over to Pilate. The allusions to that teaching contained in this scene before Annas amply suffice.[13] On the other hand, the Johannine scene of Peter's denials intriguingly suggests that the author was aware of some tradition similar to that of the Markan account. Not only do Peter's denials frame the account of the interrogation, creating a contrast between Peter and Jesus in just the same way, but there is a striking similarity of verbal detail in the triple denial: 'into the High Priest's palace . . . the servant-girl . . . Peter warming himself . . . again he denied . . . and immediately the cock crowed'. This is not enough to demand a shared written source, but it does suggest a detailed oral story – to which the author has added further details, such as the relationship of the servant to Peter's victim in the garden.

---

[13] 'The Evangelist did not find it necessary to narrate the trial before the Sanhedrin during the Passion because in the Fourth Gospel the major elements of the Sanhedrin trial occur during Jesus' public ministry', Matera, 1990, p. 54.

6

JESUS BEFORE PILATE

MARK'S ACCOUNT
Mark 15:2–20

THE INTERROGATION BY PILATE
Mark 15:2–5

Discovery of the historical facts behind the gospel account faces the same challenges as have already become evident in the discussion of earlier incidents. Were any of the disciples present? Hardly! Could they have heard from an eye-witness information which was eventually passed on to the evangelists? Are the very different accounts in the synoptic gospels and in John reconcilable? Mark has composed the scene from two elements, a dialogue between Pilate and Jesus, and the Barabbas incident. The other synoptic evangelists adapt or re-read the Markan scene to express their own theologies.

The Markan account is indelibly signed with Mark's own hand. Firstly, with plenty of Markan expressions, e.g. the favourite Markan ἐπηρώτα (occurring 8 times in Matthew, 22 times in Mark, 17 times in Luke and only twice in John) twice, each time without λέγειν,[1] and here used with the frequent Markan inaccuracy (it really means 'to question *further*' and should be used only of a second or further question, 15:2 and 4); πολλά used adverbially to mean 'much' instead of 'many things' (15:3); the ubiquitous πάλιν, 'again' (15:4); the double

---

[1] A characteristically Markan feature of usage, see C. H. Turner in Elliott, 1993, pp. 134–5.

negatives (15:4 and 5). Secondly, it has the same structure as the account of the trial before the High Priest. Verbally there is a marked similarity:

14:53 They led Jesus away (ἀπήγαγον)	15:1 They led Jesus away (ἀπήνεγκαν)
14:60 Question (ἐπηρώτα αὐτὸν)	15:2 Question (ἐπηρώτησεν αὐτὸν)
14:60 Surprise at Jesus' silence to charges	15:4 Surprise at Jesus' silence to charges
14:61 'Are you the Christ?'	15:2 'Are you the King of the Jews?'
14:62 Jesus' affirmative answer to presider	15:2 Jesus' affirmative answer to presider
14:61 Further question (πάλιν ἐπηρώτα αὐτὸν)	15:4 Further question (πάλιν ἐπηρώτα αὐτὸν)
14:61 Silence of Jesus (οὐκ ἀπεκρίνατο οὐδέν)	15:5 Silence of Jesus (οὐκ ἀπεκρίνῃ οὐδὲν)
14:65 Mockery by participants and servants	15:16–20 Mockery by soldiers

Furthermore there is the similarity of multiple ineffective accusations, Jesus' silence (after the manner of the Suffering Servant of Isaiah 53), and the fact that in each case progress can be made only through Jesus' own answer, though each process ends inconclusively, without any sentence or verdict. Nor could this little scene represent any sort of trial; it lacks any sort of legal logic. There is no explanation of why Pilate puts his pivotal first question: who has told him that Jesus is accused of being king of the Jews?[2] This makes better sense in Luke's scene, where Pilate's question could at any rate be a sardonic reaction to the accusations of kingly behaviour which Luke introduces. Why do the chief priests continue with their ineffectual and unspecified accusations? If Mark had not put first the dialogue between Pilate and Jesus over his royalty (15:2), the progression between the chief priests handing Jesus over to Pilate and their accusing him would have been logical enough. As it is, the only purposes of 15:3–5 are to parallel the previous trial, to show Jesus fulfilling the scriptural silence and to excite Pilate's wonder at his dignity. In this interrogation scene we are

---

[2] How did he get hold of it? Senior, 1975, points out (p. 225) that in Mark the title is used only by Pilate and his soldiers (15:2, 9, 12, 18, 26).

witnessing rather the expression of Mark's view of Jesus than a record
of a trial.

THE BARABBAS SCENE
Mark 15:6–15

The Barabbas incident is also fully Markan. It continues the Markan
scheme of triples (three Passion predictions, three returns to the disciples in Gethsemane, three accusations by the High Priest, three
mockeries), and shows several other Markan stylistic features
(periphrastic tenses in 15:7; ἤρξατο with infinitive in 15:8; delayed
explanation with γὰρ and a piece of psychological speculation in 15:10;
the frequent πάλιν in 15:12 and 13, cf. chapter 2, note 15). The most
obvious feature, however, is also the most Markan, the ironic structure
of the whole piece: it is as King of the Jews that Jesus is condemned.
Mark's readers accept him as King of the Jews, but it is precisely as
king that his own people reject him and prefer Barabbas. The accent
of the whole scene is to put the burden on the Jews, who are invited
by each of Pilate's questions to implicate themselves further: first, 'Do
you wish that I should release the King of the Jews?', then the even
more sarcastic, 'Then what shall I do with him whom *you* call King of
the Jews?', and finally, 'What evil has he done?' In each of these cases
Pilate is making the crowd reach a decision which is his responsibility
and make a judgement which he himself should have made: the governor
should decide on the release of a prisoner, the governor should decide
on his right to the title, and the governor should assess what evil he
has done.

Mark's manner of painting the scene does not, of course, affect its
basic historicity. No such festal amnesty of a prisoner is known anywhere in the Roman world, but Judaea was unique as a territory within
the Empire, and it would have been a fittingly conciliatory gesture on the
festival of the liberation of the Jews from slavery in Egypt. External
historical evidence neither supports nor invalidates this amnesty. Primarily, the scene shows Pilate not as a weakling but as a skilled and
wily negotiator, who managed to kill two birds with one stone, solving
the problem of both Barabbas and Jesus at one blow, and avoiding any
nationalistic trouble by persuading the people that it was their own
solution. Helen Bond expresses it neatly by calling Mark's Pilate 'a

skilful politician, manipulating the crowd to avoid a potentially difficult situation' (Bond, 1998, p. 117).

THE INTERROGATION BEFORE PILATE –
MATTHEW'S ACCOUNT
Matthew 27:1–31

It is fascinating to see how Matthew reads Mark's account from his own very Jewish point of view. He makes subtle changes, well within the conventions permitted in Jewish historical writing, which for his Jewish Christian readership bring out the lessons of the story.

MATTHEW'S TECHNIQUES
IN THE PILATE NARRATIVE

Matthew's use of dreams and scriptural allusions here are typical of Jewish writing of the time,. It would be wholly mistaken to ask where Matthew got his information about these three little incidents, the death of Judas, the dream of Pilate's wife and Pilate's hand-washing. They are all elaborations or embroidery to enable the reader better to understand the meaning of the central events. To the Jewish and scriptural mind, each 'incident' is a justified deduction: things *must* have happened this way, or, if they did not, they *should* have done. A factual record or source was quite unnecessary.

First Matthew inserts the story of the death of Judas. It falls easily into the frequent biblical genre of an aetiological story, a story to explain a name, a feature of landscape or behaviour, in this case the name *Hakeldama*, 'Field of Blood'. But it is also a midrash on at least two Old Testament texts (Zech. 11:12–13 and Jer. 39:8–15). The basic significance of Judas' suicide by hanging is to be found in the similar death of the only suicide told in the Hebrew Bible, that of Ahitophel, David's companion and counsellor. Ahitophel betrayed his master and sided with the rebel Absalom. When his wise strategy for the defeat of David was fatally rejected by young Absalom (2 Sam. 17:23), Ahitophel went off and hanged himself. However, as often, Matthew's use of the Old Testament here is quite complicated. The quotation is not from Jeremiah but from Zechariah 11:13. There is a further complication, in that the mention of the treasury in Matthew 27:6 shows that the allusion

includes two different textual readings of Zechariah 11:13, both (יוזר)
('potter') and (אוזר) ('treasury').[3] We simply do not know what readings
were current at the time Matthew wrote, before the standardisation of
the Hebrew text. Two stern details in Matthew's account must be mentioned: firstly, Judas does not repent in a way which invites forgiveness.
This is regularly described by the Greek verb μετανοέω; Matthew here
avoids this technical term for 'repentance' and uses μεταμεληθείς:
Judas simply 'changes his mind'. Secondly, Matthew takes the opportunity to mock the legalism of the chief priests and elders: their concern
not to put the price of innocent blood into the sacred treasury is
laughable when compared with the hounding of the innocent man in
itself.

The dream of Pilate's wife is similarly typically Jewish, though also
one more instance of the gentile getting it right where the Jews get it
wrong. A dream was considered one of God's ways of imparting information, a sure image of things as they are, so that this dream is an
incontrovertible assurance of the innocence of Jesus, corresponding to
the frequent oracles received in dreams in the Bible (e.g. 2 Sam. 7:4),
and indeed in Matthew's own infancy narrative (1:20; 2:13, 19). The
language of these two verses is so thoroughly Matthean that there can
be no doubt that he formed them himself.[4] The insertion serves to give
the positive divine reaction to the envy and jealousy which had
motivated the handing over of Jesus.

It is also natural for Matthew to express Pilate's denial of responsibility for the death of Jesus with the biblical gesture of washing the
hands (27:24). This is the gesture prescribed in Deuteronomy 21:6 for
the elders of a town at the end of an unsuccessful murder investigation;
it both implies Jesus' innocence and attempts to distance Pilate from
the responsibility of his condemnation. Whether Pilate would have been
sufficiently at home with Jewish customs is one question; whether
Matthew's readers would understand the implications of this gesture is
another. Matthew must also have intended an internal allusion to the
contrast between Jew and gentile in his own infancy story: just as

---

[3] Longenecker, 1975, p. 133.
[4] The introductory genitive absolute (and exactly as Matt 24:3), the speech-intro-
ducing λέγουσα, and the individual words δίκαιος, σήμερον, κατ'ὄναρ.

the gentile Magi[5] recognise the child Jesus as king, while the leader
of the Jewish nation attempts to annihilate him, so the gentile Pilate
acknowledges Jesus as king while his own people reject him. Indeed,
right from the beginning (27:13–14) Pilate's awed amazement is
stressed. Yet it is not Pilate's recognition of Jesus which finally drives
him to action, so much as fear of a loss of control (θόρυβος, riot); the
blame still lies firmly with the Jewish crowd.

THE MESSIAH REJECTED

Throughout his treatment of this scene Matthew concentrates the attention in a spine-chilling and almost brutal way on the rejection of
Jesus, precisely as Messiah, by his own people. Firstly, he removes the
motivation of Barabbas' political involvement, given in Mark 15:7.
Barabbas is now simply 'a well-known prisoner called Barabbas'. He
no longer has a nationalistic claim on their attention but is simply a
nondescript prisoner, making the crowds' choice of him less reputable.
Secondly, Matthew makes it a straight choice between Jesus and Barabbas.[6] In Mark Barabbas has been introduced but then left in the
background, so that the reader could well wonder why he has been
introduced at all. The crowd takes the initiative, to which Pilate responds
by asking whether they want 'the King of the Jews' released. Barabbas
becomes relevant only later, by a clever move of the chief priests. From
the beginning of Matthew's account, however, we are left in no doubt
that there is a straight choice in progress, an either/or (27:17), and
initiated by Pilate; the crowd has merely 'come together' not for any
particular purpose, by contrast with Mark's account, where they come
specifically to ask for the release of a prisoner. In Matthew the choice
between the two is unambiguously offered to the crowd: 'release *to the*

---

[5] The similarity leaps to mind also because the gentile Pilate (and, in imitation, his
soldiers) and the gentile Magi are the only people who call Jesus 'King of the
Jews' in Matthew.

[6] The parallel between the two figures is emphasised if the text for 27:16 is accepted
as '*Jesus* Barabbas', as in some manuscripts. Origen attests this reading as present
in several manuscripts known to him, and many modern scholars accept it. If it
were not original, it is unlikely that Christian copyists would have added the word
'Jesus', especially as 'Barabbas' is the Aramaic for 'son of the father'. See the
full discussion in Senior, 1975, p. 238, footnote 3.

crowd whom they *wanted*' (27:15), 'whom do you *want* me to release *to you?*' (27:17). Similarly, at the next stage, the chief priests and elders persuaded[7] the crowds (plural, not singular as in Mark) not merely to gain Barabbas' release, but 'to ask for Barabbas *and liquidate Jesus*' (27:20). It is not merely that Jesus will be left over if Barabbas is preferred, but they positively request Jesus' destruction. This deliberate choice is further emphasised with maximum clarity by Pilate's two separate questions, 'Whom *of the two* do you *want* me to release *to you?*' (27:21) and 'What then shall I do with Jesus *called Christ?*' (27:22). The grinding emphasis continues, 'They *all* cried out ... ' (27:22), 'they *continued to* cry out' (27:23 – Matthew neatly changes Mark's aorist to the continuous imperfect). The responsibility is already removed from Pilate by the double change of the imperative, 'Crucify him!' (Mark 15:13 and 14) to the impersonal passive, 'Let him be crucified!' (Matthew 27:22 and 23), as though Pilate had nothing to do with it.

Most significantly, Matthew clarifies that it is the Messiah they are rejecting, 'Barabbas or Jesus *called Christ*' (27:17). And it is now the crowds rather than the chief priests (as in Mark 15:10) who have handed Jesus over out of jealousy. There may also be significance in Matthew's change of verb: instead of Mark's 'he had ascertained' (ἐγίνωσκεν) Matthew has the more positive and absolute 'he knew' (ᾔδει) – he just knew for a fact. According to Matthew (27:22) Pilate again points out to them Jesus' position, 'What shall I do with Jesus *called Christ?*' (27:22) as they make the final choice.

The climax comes after the hand-washing, when Pilate challenges them and they respond deliberately and positively: '"I am innocent of this man's blood. See to it yourselves!" And the whole people replied, "His blood on us and on our children"' (27:25). The full strength of this declaration or self-curse must be appreciated. Hitherto the spectators have been designated as 'the crowd' or 'the crowds'. Now they are given emphatically the sacred title of the People of God: it is the

---

[7] There is not even the excuse that the crowd was acting irresponsibly. This will do for Mark's account, when 'the chief priests stirred up (ἀνέσεισαν) the crowd', but Matthew removes any suggestion of pardonable excitement. 'Persuaded' suggests deliberate and thoughtful acquiescence.

nation as a whole which responds, for the λαός (the technical term here used) are the People whom Yahweh chose as his own.

This cry has been so frequently and so virulently used as a theological justification for Christian persecution of Jews that it must be examined more closely in its context. Christian apologetic has so often claimed that 'they invited condemnation and vengeance on themselves'. Matthew's careful designation of 'the whole People' definitively rules out any claim that he considers only the chief priests and elders (cf. 27:20) to be implicated. Has this casual group of spectators then invited condemnation on the whole Jewish people for all time to come? Two important mitigating factors must be considered: Matthew's writing stems, as we have seen, from the situation of acute conflict towards the end of the first century between Jews who saw Jesus, the Messiah, as the fulfilment of the hope of Israel, and those who refused such an interpretation of the man. The refusal of the Jews and the entrance of the gentiles into salvation has been a concern of Matthew throughout the gospel. This appears in the contrast between Herod and the gentile Magi, in 'Galilee of the gentiles' (4:12–16), in the centurion of Capernaum (8:5–13), in the parable of the two sons (21:28–32), in the codicil to the parable of the vinedressers (21:43), and finally in the Great Commission (28:16–20). No conflict is so full of recriminations as a family conflict, and the strength of this language is mild, when compared to the language of controversy and condemnation employed in contemporary disputes between, for example, the sectaries of Qumran and their opponents.

Secondly, it must be remembered that Matthew is writing towards the end of the century. A generation after the events here described, destruction did come upon the children of those who were here speaking, in the form of the Sack of Jerusalem in AD 70. Has Matthew this particular retribution in mind? The allusion to Jeremiah contained in the words of the people may indicate that this is the case. There is a clear echo of the scene shortly before the Sack of Jerusalem in 597 BC, when Jeremiah says to 'the priests and prophets and all the people' threatening to kill him, 'But be sure of this, that if you put me to death, you will be bringing innocent blood on yourselves, on this city and on its inhabitants' (Jer. 26:15). The principal meaning of these words would then be that just as the destruction of Jerusalem in 597 BC was to be attributed to the rejection of the prophet Jeremiah, so now

the destruction of Jerusalem in the next generation was to be attributed
to the rejection of Jesus as Messiah.

After this Matthean ascription of guilt, it remains only for Matthew
to conclude the scene with a neat chiasmus, slimming down Mark's
rather bulky conclusion and again contrasting the two prisoners:

> ἀπέλυσεν τὸν Βαραββᾶν . . . τὸν Ἰησοῦν παρέδωκεν,
> 'he released Barabbas . . . Jesus he handed over'.

THE INTERROGATION BEFORE PILATE AND HEROD – LUKE'S ACCOUNT
Luke 23:1–25

Luke has very largely re-formed the Markan account to express his
own theology. This is done so consistently and coherently that there is
no need to suppose that he had any other factual source. Three ideas
guide this re-formulation:

1. CHRISTOLOGICAL

In this account Jesus is above all the teacher. In accordance with Luke's
presentation of Jesus as prophet throughout the gospel, but as teacher
especially during the Jerusalem ministry, it is for this activity that the
Jews want him condemned. 'He was teaching daily in the Temple'
brackets Jesus' ministry in Jerusalem (19:47; 21:37). It is this which
annoys the authorities. Already a subtle change from Mark's account
took place in the challenge by the Temple authorities in 20:1–2: Jesus
had been teaching and evangelising in the Temple, so that 'Tell us on
what authority you do this' (20:2) instead of referring, as it does in
Mark 11:28, to the cleansing of the Temple, refers to Jesus' teaching.
The charge of destruction of the Temple remains, as it did in Luke's
version of the Jewish hearing, well in the background. Correspondingly,
the political charge of claiming to be King of the Jews remains only
in 23:2–3. The centre of interest is the teaching of Jesus.

It has often been remarked that Luke, the careful historian, insists
that there must be charges mentioned, rather than allowing Pilate, as
Mark does, simply to sail unmotivated and uninformed into the charge,
'Are you the King of the Jews?' (Mark 15:2). Who, as we asked earlier,

has told Pilate of this claim? The three charges which Luke mentions are, of course, false, but the important aspect is that they all concern Jesus' teaching.

- 'We have found this man leading the people astray' (23:2) – but the reader knows that the people are already astray (9:41).
- 'opposing payment of tribute to Caesar' – this would be a good charge to bring before any Roman governor, but again the pericope on tribute (20:20–26) has shown it to be false.
- 'claiming to be Christ, a king' – again, a good political charge, which in fact has never been part of Jesus' teaching in Luke. 'Are you the Christ?' was the first of the questions put to Jesus in the preliminary hearing, and Jesus in Luke is primarily the prophet-messiah, not a king. The modified charge is, however, necessary to lead into Pilate's question. It is the only time the kingship appears in Luke's account of the trials. In the mockery by Herod Luke has carefully avoided this implication (23:11): no suggestion of imperial purple robe, of crown or of sceptre. In the rest of the trial this charge lies neglected.

Similarly, when the opponents of Jesus return to the charge, the charge is that he is 'inflaming the people with his teaching all over Judaea and all the way from Galilee' (23:5). When Pilate declares Jesus innocent a second time, this is the charge he refutes: 'You brought this man before me as turning the people away' (23:14), again a matter of Jesus' teaching.

2. RESPONSIBILITY

Each of the synoptic evangelists has his own angle on the responsibility for Jesus' condemnation. The Markan account showed Pilate actively shifting the responsibility onto the Jews. The Matthean account concentrated on the Jewish people rejecting their own Messiah. The Lukan account shows the Jewish authorities and people determinedly egging Pilate on to condemn Jesus, Pilate himself fighting an unsuccessful rearguard action. 'The entire scene is composed in order to emphasise the responsibility of priests, rulers and people' (Matera, 1989, p. 549). There are two points to note.

1. The strength of Luke's language is striking. 'They persisted' (23:5); 'but as one man they howled' (23:18); 'they shouted back' (23:21); the single cry of Mark, 'Crucify!' is doubled and put in the more pressing present tense; 'but they kept on shouting at the top of their voices, demanding that he should be crucified. And their shouts kept growing louder' (23:23). In counterpoint, it is to their demand that Pilate accedes: far from condemning Jesus, he three times, in equally strong language, declares Jesus' innocence: 'I find no case against this man' (23:4); 'I have found no grounds in the man for any of the charges you bring against him – and nor did Herod' (23:14); 'I have found no case against him that deserves death' (23:22). At the mid-point Pilate, while protesting Jesus' innocence, feebly and illogically suggests a beating, an admonitory thrashing rather than the brutal and often fatal scourging which was the first stage of crucifixion (the Greek παιδεύω really means 'to teach a lesson', quite different from the φραγέλλω which occurs in the other accounts). In the end Pilate does not condemn him, but goes no further than 'he gave his verdict that their demand was to be granted' (23:24). The further motivation for this emphasis is still a matter for debate. Is Luke attempting to show that the followers of Jesus pose no threat to Rome and its government, an *apologia* for Christianity addressed to Romans? Or is he showing that Rome poses no threat to the followers of Jesus, an *apologia* for Rome to Christians?[8] Or is he – more complicatedly – showing that, although Rome was well inclined towards Christianity, it was badly served by weak governors?[9]

2. Luke insists that the whole people is involved. This is surprising, for hitherto Luke has been careful to show a contrast between the people and their leaders. The leaders had been hostile, the people favourable. Now the situation has changed: in the early speeches of Acts the 'Men of Israel' are blamed squarely for demanding the death of Jesus (Acts 3:13; 4:27; 13:28). In the Passion Narrative itself Luke leaves no doubt: at the preliminary hearing in 22:66 he adds to Mark's account 'the elders *of the people*' as gathered together. Similarly ἅπαν τὸ πλῆθος ('the whole number'), who

---

[8] This is the thesis of Walaskay, 1983.
[9] Bond, 1998, p. 142.

lead Jesus away to Pilate, suggests not merely the number of the elders, chief priests and scribes, but the whole gang of the people. It is they who produce the accusations and continuously play an active role. Pilate replies to 'the chief priests *and the crowds*' (23:4). In Pilate's next scene he 'calls together the chief priests and the rulers *and the people*' (23:13). In the final verses the only purpose of the appearance of Barabbas is to whip the crowd up to greater insistence. Finally it is the vociferous fury of the crowd which wins the day παμπληθεὶ ('in full number', 23:18). Is all this preparing for the repentance which will occur at the cross?

3. THE DISCIPLES UNDER PERSECUTION

The Church of his own day is constantly in Luke's mind, and, as so often in the gospel, Jesus serves as a model for his disciples under persecution. His followers will be brought before kings and governors 'for the sake of my name' (Luke 21:12), so it is suitable that Jesus himself should be brought before both a governor and a king. Similarly in the story of Paul the Herodian King Agrippa is brought in to give his verdict on Paul (Acts 25:14), just as his uncle Herod Antipas was brought in to give his verdict on Jesus. The innocence of Paul will there be stressed (Acts 23:29; 25:25; 26:31; 28:18), just as Jesus' innocence here.

The scene requires no separate factual source; it is constructed with typical Lukan art and skill, for Luke is a master at constructing such little scenes in order to express theological truths (e.g. the disciples on the road to Emmaus, Peter's release from prison in Acts 12). The vocabulary and literary style are unmistakably characteristic of Luke in his most sophisticated mode, as befits a story about a hellenistic monarch. Luke shows his knowledge of Roman legislation by allowing Pilate to seize on the mention of Galilee to suggest that Jesus should be tried according to his *forum domicilii*.[10] Herod's satisfaction at seeing Jesus (23:8) links back artistically to his anxiety to see Jesus already expressed in 9:9, and his dilettante buffoonery with Jesus stands in

---

[10] See Sherwin-White, 1963, pp. 28–31. A criminal could be tried either in his *forum delicti* (the court where the crime had been committed) or in his *forum domicilii* (the court where his domicile was).

sharp contrast to his earlier desire to kill Jesus (13:31) as further evidence of Jesus' innocence. Typical of Luke also is the comment that Herod and Pilate were reconciled to each other (23:12): even in his own moment of trial Jesus brings healing of enmity. Otherwise Luke composes the scene by mopping up other elements of Mark and adapting them to his own view: Jesus' silence at the charges (23:9) is transferred from Mark 15:4. The insistent accusations of chief priests and scribes (23:10) are taken from Mark 15:3. The mockery by Herod and his soldiery (23:11) replaces and mitigates that of the Roman soldiers in Mark 15:16–20. There is, however, as we have noted, no suggestion of kingship, purple robe, crown, sceptre or genuflexion, and the more humiliating aspects of spitting and buffeting are omitted.

JESUS BEFORE PILATE IN JOHN
John 18:28–19:24

A CLIMAX OF JOHANNINE THEMES

As will become apparent, the section-title 'Jesus before Pilate' is only superficially apt. Just as in the Annas scene it was questionable who was interrogating whom, so now it is questionable whether Pilate is judging Jesus or Jesus Pilate and others. Two themes which have been running parallel, and often intertwined, throughout the gospel here reach their climax, namely the revelation of Jesus' identity and the theme of judgement. The whole gospel may be viewed as one great judgement scene, for forensic terms appear constantly: truth and falsehood, judge, judgement, witness, bear witness, advocate.

Throughout the gospel of John the person of Jesus has been being revealed. This is one of the major distinctions between the synoptic gospels and John: in the former Jesus is proclaiming the reign of God, concentrating on God, with little attention to himself; in the latter he is revealing himself. In the synoptics Jesus says little about himself, and most of what he does say is hidden under the self-description as 'son of man'; in John the ἐγώ εἰμι ('I am') sayings are of paramount importance. The kingdom of God, so central in the synoptics, is mentioned only twice (John 3:3, 5), for John uses as its equivalent 'eternal life' (which barely occurs in the synoptic gospels), which is to be

obtained in and through Jesus. The explicit revelation starts immediately. During the first days in the Jordan Valley one title after another
is given to Jesus as each of the disciples comes to him (1:35–50). The
Baptist leads off by announcing him with the mysterious title 'Lamb
of God'. With Johannine irony the reader knows all too well, but the
actors in the scene are still unable to penetrate, that this refers to Jesus
as the Paschal lamb. Then the two disciples call him simply 'Rabbi',
then Andrew hails him as 'Messiah'. Then Philip calls him 'the one
about whom Moses in the Law and the prophets spoke'. Nathanael
brings this to a climax with 'Son of God and King of Israel'. Even this
is not enough, for 'You will see greater things than that' (1:50).

From then on the progressive revelation occurs, and the witnesses
judge themselves by their confrontation with Jesus and their reaction
of acceptance or rejection. We see being carried out the process
announced by Jesus: 'The Father judges no one; he has entrusted all
judgement to the Son', and 'whoever listens to my words and believes
in the one who sent me has eternal life and has passed from death to
life' (5:22, 24). Hence, at the marriage feast of Cana, at the forestalled
'hour' (again an ominous, ironic hint) the disciples see his glory and
believe in him, while immediately afterwards 'the Jews', rejecting the
sign of the new Temple which he offers them, start off on their disastrous downward spiral. Nicodemus comes by night and remains sitting
on the fence for the time being. Next the Samaritan woman, for all
her initial freshness and impertinence, receives with enthusiasm the
revelation that Jesus is the Messiah. Then begin the great oppositions
as the witnesses of revelation divide and go simultaneously in opposite
directions. The man cured at the Pool of Bethesda commits himself to
Jesus, while the Jews want to kill Jesus for the blasphemy of speaking
of God as his Father. At the bread of life discourse even some of the
disciples judge themselves by refusing to accept the message of
the living bread. At the Festival of Shelters the revelation of Jesus
continues, as the living water and the light of the world, but the Jews
respond only with disbelief and the attempt to stone Jesus. The cure of
the man born blind shows the Jews pushing the cured man towards
Jesus by their very attempts to curb his belief. Finally Jesus' gift of
life to Lazarus leads many to acknowledge him, but the chief priests
and Pharisees only to make the final decision to kill him – with typical

Johannine opposition, the gift of life leads directly to the option for death.[11]

The discourse after the Last Supper has made clear that the hour of Jesus is the moment of full revelation, for the priestly prayer (John 17) is bracketed by 'Father, glorify your Son so that your Son may glorify you' and 'I have made your name known and will continue to make it known, so that the love with which you loved me may be in them' (John 17:1, 26). The judgement-scene is one of the great moments of this revelation.

THE ARTISTRY OF THE SCENE

The Chiasmus

The Greek letter *chi* (written 'X') gives its name to a pattern common in ancient and especially biblical literature (e.g. Matt. 23:16–22), a pattern of concentric opposites, of which the climax is normally the central element, with a secondary climax at the end (see chapter 1, note 21). In this scene the basic shape is given by the alternation of action outside and inside the Praetorium. This brings into prominence the absurd irony of the fussy adherence by the Jews to purity regulations – in refusing to enter the Praetorium – while they are engineering a far greater injustice than ritual defilement.

18:28 The Jews demand death	outside
18:33 Pilate questions Jesus	inside
18:38 Jesus declared innocent	outside
19:2 JESUS CROWNED KING	inside
19:4 Jesus declared innocent	outside
19:9 Pilate questions Jesus	inside
19:13 Jews obtain death: WE HAVE NO KING BUT CAESAR	outside

The central element is therefore the scourging, mockery and crowning of Jesus. As we have seen, the scourging has occurred differently in the accounts of Mark/Matthew and of Luke. In the former it was the

---

[11] Such dualism occurs throughout the gospel: 1:11–12 acceptance >< non-acceptance; 3:6 flesh >< spirit; 3:19 light >< darkness; 8:23 above >< below; 8:44 truth >< lies; 9:39 sight >< blindness. 'John had dualism in his bones', says Ashton, 1991, p. 237.

cruel preliminary to execution, in the latter a lighter, admonitory form of correction. In all the synoptics, however, it occurs only at the end of or after Pilate's judgement. In John it occurs illogically, half-way through the proceedings, when the scourging has no legal justifi-cation and the mockery constitutes an untimely interruption. John must have had a non-historical reason for so displacing it, namely to bring into prominence the kingship of Jesus through the chiasmus which he builds.

Jesus' royal dignity is one of the keys to John's presentation of the hour, the moment of exaltation of Jesus, which sounds again and again throughout the narrative. The dialogue between Jesus and Pilate in the first half of the chiasmus (18:33–39) is centred upon the explanation of what kind of kingship it is, kingship not of this world, but a king-ship of witness to the truth. Pilate writes himself off by his contempt for truth, merely throwing out the careless question, 'What is truth?' and not even waiting for an answer. Once Jesus has been crowned and mocked as king – again, Johannine irony, for the unwitting soldiery mock him for what we know to be true – there is a still more positive exegesis of what this means. The Jews themselves brazenly inform Pilate of Jesus' claim to be Son of God, which at any rate fills Pilate with awe and fear. The picture is completed by the movement of the dialogue to the source of Jesus' authority. Jesus' enigmatic answer fills Pilate with yet more dread. The final stage then comes with Pilate bringing out Jesus and seating him on the judgement seat.[12] It is then before Jesus, crowned as king and enthroned as judge, that the Jews abjure themselves with the dreadful cry, 'We have no king but Caesar.'

---

[12] The Greek verb καθίζω can be either transitive or intransitive, so that 19:13 can be translated either 'Pilate led out Jesus and sat down on the judgement seat' or 'Pilate led out Jesus and sat him down on the judgement seat'. The expression is used twice in the New Testament in this form, of God *seating* Jesus at his right hand (Acts 2:34; Eph. 1:20), so both times transitively. It is standard Greek grammar that the object of two verbs, if given after the first, need not be repeated after the second, and it is certainly in accordance with John's style to omit the repeated object ('him') in a second limb of a sentence. The historical improba-bility of Pilate seating Jesus on the judgement seat is lessened if it is not a throne but e.g. a mere stone bench. In any case, the author is a theologian, giving an impression of Jesus, rather than a chronicler recording facts. It is typical of John to make use of ambiguity in this way, stating one thing and suggesting another (cf. born *anew* or *from above*, 3:3; living water or the water of life, 4:10–15).

If Judaism does not recognise Yahweh as King, the sole King, it no longer has a reason to exist, for this is at the heart of the hopes of Israel, its psalms and liturgy, and its expectation of the kingship to come. They are declaring the total bankruptcy of their position.

Finally the universal kingship of Jesus is again stressed by the *titulus* on the cross (19:19–22). This is mentioned also by the other evangelists (Mark 15:26), and indeed it was normal for the offence of the executed criminal to be thus placarded, as a deterrent to other possible offenders, but John emphasises it. It is proclaimed to all by being written in the three world languages. Against the Jews' expostulation that it should be phrased as a mere claim, Pilate insists that it should remain expressed as the truth.

The Tone of the Dialogue

The whole tone of the dialogues is truculent and mocking. The Jews' first reply to Pilate is cheeky, 'If he were not a criminal, we should not have handed him over to you' (18:30). Pilate's reply to this is mocking, to which the Jews unhelpfully reply with the assumption that Jesus is guilty of a capital offence, 'We are not allowed to put a man to death' (18:31). Similarly Jesus speaks past Pilate, not answering either of his questions ('Are you the King of the Jews?' and 'What have you done?'), and finally elaborating quite gratuitously on witness to the truth when he has been asked about kingship. Pilate then mocks the Jews further by offering to release to them by amnesty the very man they have asked him to execute (18:39); he rubs it in by personalising it and by the title, 'release *for you* the King of the Jews'. Similarly after the central scene, Pilate again mocks the Jews by telling them, 'Take him yourselves and crucify him', knowing full well that they have no right to do so. Jesus also continues to speak past Pilate, not answering his question about authority, but returning with a statement about the source of this authority (19:11). Finally Pilate again mocks the Jews by implying that they accept Jesus as king, 'Shall I crucify your king?' (19:15). Despite dismissing the case, Pilate's tone to Jesus is mocking too, from the sneer, 'Am I a Jew?', to the throw-away line 'What is truth?' and the final 'Are you refusing to speak to me?'

The whole interchange is uncomfortable and adversarial, but not uncharacteristic of Johannine dialogue. One might expect sarcasm from the opponents of Jesus (4:12; 7:27; 8:53, 57; 10:33), but it is no less typical of the disciples (1:46; 11:16) and even of Jesus himself (3:10; 7:23; 13:38; 16:31). Like ambiguity and duality, it is one of the characteristics of the Johannine style. Other such adversarial and slightly inconsequential dialogues are not uncommon, e.g. 7:20–30; 8:13–30, 39–58.

7

THE CRUCIFIXION

MARK'S ACCOUNT

It is convenient to divide this final scene in the Passion Narrative into four elements, the crucifixion itself (15:22–27), the mockeries (15:29–32), the death of Jesus (15:33–37) and its consequences (15:38–41). Before and after, however, the scene is locked in by witnesses, first Simon of Cyrene (15:21), the mention of whose sons Alexander and Rufus suggests that they were known to Mark's audience. There would have been many Cyreneans scattered round the Roman world, and these are common enough names. Acts 6:9 mentions Cyrenian members of a Jerusalem synagogue. At the end are mentioned the women who had followed him from Galilee (15:40–41). This is a typical Markan envelope, framing the scene.

Typical also is the pattern of three (three divisions of time, three mockeries, three reactions to Jesus' death). Further than this, there are curious instances of Markan duality about the account, two mentions of drink offered (15:23, 36), two mentions of the actual crucifying (15:24, 25), two loud cries (15:34, 37). The duality of the first and last pairs is, however, unlike the usual instances of Markan duality, where one element immediately follows the other ('at evening / when the sun had set'; 'when David was in need / and was hungry'), in that each of the pairs is separated. The double mention of crucifixion corresponds more nearly to the usual, resumptive pattern. Are the other instances different traditions of the same event, used differently? The first drink offered out of pity and refused by Jesus is a mild narcotic. The second, the rough, peasant, vinegary wine may be a taunt, for in Psalm 69:21 and the Qumran Scrolls the offer of vinegar to drink is ascribed to enemies:

> They [the teachers of lies and seers of falsehood] withhold from
> the thirsty the drink of knowledge and assuage their thirst with
> vinegar' (1QH 4:11).

Of the two cries, the first is important as putting on Jesus' lips the intonation of the Psalm which gives the meaning of the Passion (see p. 125), while the second seems to lack any theological interpretation.

THE CRUCIFIXION

This description is remarkable as much for what it does not say as for what it does. There is no dwelling on the horrors of this barbaric method of execution. It was too familiar in the Roman world, and as long as it remained so, realistic representations of the crucifixion were avoided in favour of a bejewelled cross. The accent is all on the theological meaning of the scene. A. Vanhoye, 1967, fittingly comments,

> The death on the cross is not seen as a failure, soon to be wiped out by the victory of the resurrection; it is not seen as an unhappy episode to be hastily forgotten. On the contrary, it constitutes a positive completion which, fulfilling the scriptures, reveals the person and crowns the work of Jesus (p. 162).

Nor is Mark precise about the location of Golgotha; the associations of the name are more important that the topographical details.

Only three features are important to Mark. In accordance with his careful principles of chronological organisation and his interest in numbers, he divides the day into periods of three hours, third, sixth, ninth hour and evening.[1] There are two principal features. Fulfilment of scripture has been a continuous interest and at this climactic moment it is intensified: the wine mixed with myrrh is mentioned not because of its supposed narcotic qualities but because it fulfils Psalm 69:21b.[2] The division of Jesus' clothes is mentioned not to draw attention to the shame of nakedness but because it fulfils Psalm 22:18. The criminals crucified on either side of Jesus are mentioned partly because they fulfil Isaiah 53:12. (Secondary manuscripts and some versions draw attention

---

[1] There is no indication that this is to accord with the Jewish hours of prayer in the Temple.

[2] Brown, 1994, however, prefers the explanation that Mark inserts this first offering of wine 'to signal to the reader Jesus' refusal of what would spare him from suffering and thus to show at the final stage of the drama Jesus' willingness to drink the cup of suffering the Father had given him' (p. 944).

to this by 15:28, but the verse is missing in the principal manuscripts, and is widely rejected.)

Markan irony gives these criminals another sense too, attached to the other principal point: the central point of the Roman trial was the claim (however derived) that Jesus was King of the Jews. It was as King of the Jews that Jesus was handed over to be crucified, and this irony now reaches its completion. There is further Markan irony in the two criminals being the sole supporters of the King of the Jews. The reader of Mark's gospel will surely also remember that, after the third solemn prediction of the Passion, the sons of Zebedee asked for a place at his right and his left 'in his glory' (10:37); it is another Markan reminder of the failure of the disciples to understand and a reminder of what his glory is.

THE MOCKERIES

The two chief mockeries (that of the criminals is a mere tailpiece, to show what sort of supporters they are), focus on the two accusations of the Jewish hearing, the charge of renewing the Temple and of being the Christ. To these is added again the charge, King of the Jews, brought before Pilate. It is notable that Mark holds back the title 'son of God' till later; it is for him the climax. The irony is intensified by the reader's knowledge both that Jesus is taunted for what he really is, and that Jesus could come down from the cross. Above all, in both cases the mockery centres on the word 'save', which the reader knows has been used so often in the stories of Jesus' ministry with the Christian overtones of saving from more than physical disability: in each of these stories the Christian reader could understand the healing or saving as an image of the ultimate salvation brought by Jesus.

THE DEATH OF JESUS

In Mark the actual death of Jesus is recounted neutrally, but its sense is given beforehand by three scriptural links. First comes the darkness at noon. Vain attempts are occasionally made to interpret this historically. It is now well enough known that no eclipse in fact took place at any time at which the event of the crucifixion can be located, but still explanations such as the eerie occurrence of a spring dust-storm (which in fact does block out the sun) are postulated. However, the immediate association of darkness at noon must be the foreboding threats of the Day of the Lord in Amos 5:20, 'Will not the Day of Yahweh be darkness not light, totally dark, without a ray of light?' and more especially Amos 8:9, 'On that Day, declares the Lord Yahweh, I shall make the sun go down at noon and darken the earth in broad daylight.' This darkness at the sixth hour therefore announces that the Day of the Lord is occurring, that great and terrible day when the judgement and restoration of Yahweh are to be manifest. From the time of Amos onwards this Day had been a marker of increasing importance in the Bible. First it was awaited with threatening fear as the Day when Israel's sins, infidelities and desertions would be avenged. Once this had occurred in the disaster of the Sack of Jerusalem by the Babylonians and the Exile, it became seen as the day of Restoration, when the Lord would punish Israel's tormentors and restore Israel to its own land. This was painted in more and more cosmic terms, terminology originally drawn from Israel's awesome experience of God on Sinai at the covenant, when God, represented in imagery of cloud, thunder, lightning and earthquake, made Israel a chosen people, bound to him for ever. With Israel's increasing awareness of universalism, that is, of Israel's mission to bring salvation to all nations, this language came to be expanded to involve astral and cosmic phenomena:

The earth quakes, the skies tremble, the stars lose their brilliance,
    Yahweh's voice rings out at the head of his troops.

(Joel 2:10)

I shall cover the skies and darken the stars,
    I shall cover the sun with clouds and the moon will not give
      its light.
    I shall dim every luminary in heaven because of you.

(Ezek. 32:7–8)

The other scriptural key given to the death of Jesus is the intonation of Psalm 22, which has featured so widely in the Passion Narrative. It has often been taken as a cry of despair, even (tentatively) by E. P.

Sanders.[3] On this sort of interpretation have been built theologies of Jesus suffering the pains of the damned, of total separation from God, even of God vengefully exacting from his Son the penalties which were due from all humankind. A less clumsy reading is to see it on the lips of the dying Jesus as the intonation implying the whole psalm. It is the clue which binds together all the other allusions to the psalm. The thrust of Psalm 22 is the achievement of the glory of God and the vindication of the sufferer only after the psalmist has passed through shame, humiliation and torture. The psalm ends in triumph:

> The whole wide world will remember and return to Yahweh,
>> all the families of nations bow down before him. . .
> Those who are dead, their descendants will serve him,
>> will proclaim his name to generations still to come. . .
>
> (Ps. 22:27–31)

The misunderstanding of the Aramaic cry is a surprising detail, involving a double contortion of Aramaic. Firstly, it does not seem possible to find any pronunciation of the Aramaic 'Elohi' which could be misunderstood as 'Eli'. Secondly, this is not in fact any short form of the name of the prophet Eliyahu. This suggests that the whole misunderstanding springs from a time when or a context where Aramaic was not understood. Nevertheless, it does serve two purposes: it provides the opportunity for one more cruel mockery of the dying man, and it strengthens the impression of the end time, for the coming of Elijah was associated with that moment, 'Look, I shall send you the prophet Elijah before the great and awesome Day of the Lord comes' (Mal. 3:1).

THE VEIL OF THE TEMPLE AND THE CENTURION

These two commentaries complete the picture of the event. It may be doubted whether either of them is meant strictly historically. It is hard

---

[3] 'My guess is that Jesus' cry was his own reminiscence of the psalm, not just a motif inserted by the early Christians. It is possible that, when Jesus drank his last cup of wine and predicted that he would drink it again in the kingdom, he thought that the kingdom would arrive immediately. After he had been on the cross a few hours, he despaired, and cried out that he had been forsaken', Sanders, 1993, pp. 274–5.

to believe that Christians continued to go to the Temple in the early
days of Acts (Acts 2:46) without any comment on the shredded veil.
The symbolic meaning is paramount, signifying that the uniqueness of
Judaism had come to an end and that the privileges of Judaism are now
open to the world. The meaning of this event is well commented by
the interpretation of a similar story in Josephus (*War*, 6.293–6) of
various phenomena presaging the destruction of the Temple by the
Romans. Included among these is the miraculous opening of the gate
of the Temple:

> The eastern gate of the inner court of the Temple, which was of
> brass and vastly heavy, and had been with difficulty shut by 20
> men, and rested upon a basis armed with iron, and had bolts
> fastened very deep into the firm floor, which was there made of
> one single stone, was seen to be opened of its own accord about
> the sixth hour of the night . . . The men of learning understood
> that the security of their holy house was dissolved of its own
> accord and the gate was opened for the advantage of their enemies.
> So these publicly declared that this signal foreshowed the
> desolation that was coming upon them.

The lesson is reinforced by the centurion's acknowledgement. The
theme of 'son of God' has run through the gospel right from the
beginning. It is in the heading, 'The beginning of the gospel of Jesus
Christ, son of God'. In Mark's introduction the expression crucially
sets the scene, showing how the gospel is to be understood. The
manuscript evidence is not wholly secure for the last three words, but
the same declaration of how Jesus is to be understood is provided
by the Voice from heaven at the Baptism (1:11), the conclusion of the
introduction. The unclean spirits cast out by Jesus have acknowledged
him as 'son of God', but this was directed at the reader rather than the
witnesses of the exorcisms, for none of the bystanders seem to react to
it. The twin titles of the heading, 'Christ' and 'son of God', dominate
the development of Mark's presentation of Jesus. Eventually Peter
brings the first great revelation of the gospel to its conclusion with his
recognition of Jesus as the Christ (8:29), but still he does not rise to
the second title. This comes onto the stage of human discussion at the
Jewish hearing with the High Priest's question and Jesus' answer, but

it is still only now that any human being acknowledges Jesus as son of God.

It is of the highest significance to Mark that this emphatic ('truly') acknowledgement comes from a gentile. There is no doubt room for irony, since the declaration can be understood on two levels: Mark was of course aware that on the lips of a gentile centurion 'son of god' would have a lesser import than to a Christian. 'Son of god' in gentile discourse would signify the special patronage of and participation with the pagan deities, whose divinity was of a distinctly lower order than that of the God of the Bible. It was used fairly freely of great men and heroes of the past, and by this time was a regular part of the Roman Emperor's title.[4] The major significance comes, however, from the fact that during his ministry Mark has shown Jesus in contact with one gentile only. The story of the Syro-Phoenician (7:24–30) shows that Jesus was open to the entry of gentiles into his company, for she wins the cure of her daughter by standing up to Jesus' abrasive put-down with a smart and cheeky retort. The case remains unique, however, until this moment, when a gentile, rather than a Jew, becomes the first human being to acknowledge Jesus as son of God. Especially in conjunction with the splitting of the Temple veil, Mark is concerned to show that with the death of Jesus the mission to the gentiles begins, and that the gentiles will be more open to the message than the original hearers of the Good News.

It begins now to be clear why the disciples have been forbidden to spread the message 'until the son of man had risen from the dead' (9:9). The vindication of Jesus by the resurrection is yet to come, but the meaning of the relationship 'son of God' begins to be clear. To be son of God demanded the full obedience to the will of the Father shown in the acceptance of suffering and death. The cry of the centurion shows an appreciation both of the relationship of son to Father, and also that the Father is not wholly divorced from the suffering of the world. In everyday speech we might say, 'He really is the son of his father', when we see a son behaving according to well-known

---

[4] It might be useful to recall that in 1964 the King of Nepal was declared a god on reaching his 18th birthday. Being at that time a schoolboy at a British public school, the King was then excused from attending chapel, on the grounds that it was inappropriate for one deity to worship another.

behaviour-patterns of his father, or especially when a son determinedly carries out his father's plans in the face of major difficulties. Thus the death of Jesus is the climax of the Incarnation, revealing in human form something of the divine. To appreciate the exact flavour of the declaration, and the still not fully articulate nature of Mark's Christology, it is important to be aware that the centurion says neither, 'this man was *a* son of God' (which would be υἱός τις τοῦ θεοῦ) nor 'this man was *the* son of God' (which would be ὁ υἱὸς τοῦ θεοῦ). Mark is not asserting that Jesus was, in Johannine terms, the incarnate Son of God, but neither is the acclamation restricted to being one son of God among many.

MATTHEW'S ACCOUNT

Matthew is careful in his account, making a number of minor changes. He adjusts the mention of Simon of Cyrene, removing the reference to his two sons (who were presumably unknown to his particular audience), and interestingly also the Markan reference to his 'coming from the fields': did he consider that this meant that he had been breaking the Law by working in the fields on the feast day?

Arrived at the place of execution, the use of scripture is intensified. Matthew changes Mark's narcotic 'wine mixed with myrrh' to 'wine mixed with gall'. This is a more obvious fulfilment of the psalm (Ps. 69:21a), but rather less likely, since gall is a positive poison; in the psalm it is given deliberately to poison an enemy. Is it out of courtesy, then, that Jesus tastes it before declining?

The chief changes that Matthew makes to the scene are two:

1. THE MOCKERY

In his account of the mockery of Jesus on the cross, Matthew makes clear references back to the Jewish investigation, stressing that what is now happening is the fulfilment of that scenario. The chief priests taunt Jesus with the same words as the High Priest had used, 'if you are the son of God' (26:63 and 27:40). This is the very taunt levelled at Jesus twice by the devil in the story of the testing in the desert (4:3, 6). The importance of this title to Matthew is clear in that the mocking priests repeat the taunt, 'for he said, "I am son of God"'; there is no doubt that for Matthew this claim is the reason why he is being crucified. The mockery is made more sardonic by their promise to believe in Jesus – not merely as Mark's 'let him come down so that we may see and believe', but a full-blooded promise, 'let him come down and we *shall* believe in him'. Matthew combines with Psalm 22 a second quotation. The crass enmity of the mockers is made clear by their use of the very words which the mocking godless use against the upright man in the Book of Wisdom 2:17–20:

> Let us see if what he says is true, and test him to see what sort of end he will have. For if the upright man is God's son, God will help him and rescue him from the clutches of his enemies. Let us condemn him to a shameful death, since God will rescue him – or so he claims.

The irony of their own situation is increased by their direct confession. 'He *is* the King of Israel' (27:42), not merely, as in Mark, sarcastically alluding to the title, but directly asserting it.

Another malicious little touch comes in 27:49: in Mark one of the bystanders offers Jesus the spongeful of rough wine, surely a helpful gesture of sympathy. At the same time he cloaks his act of kindness with the sarcastic remark, 'Leave him be [plural]! Let's see if Elijah comes to take him down'. In Matthew there is a contrast between the person who offers the rough wine and 'the others' who sadistically forbid this gesture of kindness. 'Leave him alone [singular]! Let's see if Elijah comes to save him.'

2. THE APOCALYPTIC SIGNS

Mark already highlights the significance of the moment by the apocalyptic phenomenon of darkness at noon. Matthew increases this dramatically. The first touch is a careful little and otherwise meaningless change in 27:45 from Mark's ὅλην to πᾶσαν, in order to introduce an allusion to the darkness over the whole land of Egypt for three days (the same figure as the three hours) as one of the Egyptian plagues (Exodus 10:22), an apocalyptic sign reminiscent of Israel's divine release from slavery.

After the death of Jesus, however, the splitting of the veil of the Temple is echoed by a proliferation of cosmic phenomena, an earthquake and the splitting of the rocks. It is notable that all the four phenomena added to Mark's account by Matthew in 27:51b–52 are described by an aorist passive: 'and the earth *was* shaken and the rocks *were* split and the tombs *were* opened and the bodies of the holy ones who had fallen asleep *were* raised'. These passives bind the four together into a little quatrain; they are no doubt theological passives by which the mention of the name of God is avoided. They constitute a typically Matthean equivalent to 'God shook the earth, split the rocks, opened the tombs and raised the bodies of the holy ones who had fallen asleep'. The first two phenomena are stock events indicating the visitation of God on the great Day of the Lord (Jer. 4:23–24; Joel 2:10; Zech. 14:4). The opening of the tombs and the raising of the dead form the fulfilment of the eschatological promise in Ezekiel 37:12–13, 'And you will know that I am Yahweh when I open your graves and raise you from your graves, my people.' Normally in the New Testament 'the holy ones' are the members of the Church, but here of course it refers to the saintly ones of the People of God among the Jews who have gone before. The phenomena form a commentary on the significance of the event which has taken place, for the general resurrection was expected (except by the Sadducees) to be part of the phenomena of the end time. In Christianity it has become the basis of the wonderful, dramatic presentations of the harrowing of Hell, those great Byzantine mosaics of the Risen Christ grasping Adam by the hand to draw him from his grave, and the article of the Creed on the descent into Hell. So also the entry into the holy city.

This entry must be into the heavenly Jerusalem, rather than the earthly Jerusalem, for Matthew can hardly have intended his readers to understand that the revived dead sauntered casually round the earthly city of Jerusalem. Nor is there any local restriction of the risen dead indicated: it is not merely representatives of the saintly dead around the earthly Jerusalem who are raised. Rather Matthew seems to envisage the general resurrection of the saintly dead. 'Many' in the second phrase could suggest a considerable but limited group, but in the first phrase it is '*the* tombs' which were opened, not '*some of* the tombs'. The 'many' therefore signifies a huge number, just as in the vision of Ezekiel. Not surprisingly, there is an awkwardness of timing; this is indicated by 27:53. They were raised on the Friday but did not enter the holy city until Sunday. What did they do meanwhile?

The raising of the dead is a sort of proleptic sign of the general resurrection of the just, wrought by the death of Jesus, but it would obviously be unfitting that their entry into the holy city should anticipate the achievement of Jesus' goal. Raymond Brown, 1994, regards the verse as 'an erudite improvement' (p. 1130) to solve the problem.

In reaction to all this, the centurion *and those with him* (not in Mark), actually witnessing the phenomena, are struck with a divine fear. They all join in the acknowledgement of Jesus as son of God.

LUKE'S ACCOUNT

Luke, brilliant raconteur that he is, tidies up what obviously seems to him Mark's somewhat sprawling and repetitive account. More important, he focuses it differently in several important respects. Particularly he takes the accent off the horror of the scene and puts it on the sovereign control of Jesus and on the salvific effects of his loving concern.

THE FRAMEWORK

First of all Luke gives a double framework to this all-important event, a framework consisting of the disciples and of the crowds. In contrast to Mark's account, where the chosen disciples have fled for their lives and are nowhere to be seen, Luke starts with the framework of Simon of Cyrene. Simon is subtly changed. Instead of being 'pressed into service' according to the authority which Roman officials had over provincials, he is simply 'grabbed'. But he carries the cross 'behind Jesus'; this is the only gospel where Simon is specifically said to carry the cross 'behind Jesus'. Such is the function of the true disciple, to join with Jesus and follow behind him in all things. Then the concluding frame at the end shows 'all those known to him' (23:49) standing watch, as well as the women who had followed from Galilee, with the suggestion that the disciples, faithless in Mark and Matthew, had remained loyal to the end. This first frame, then, fixes the disciples in the picture at the beginning and end of the crucifixion scene, and so present throughout the scene. In addition there are two little hints which show that Luke may well have had in mind the touching scene of Abraham sacrificing his son, Isaac: at 23:26 'they laid upon him' the cross, using the same verb as is used when Abraham 'laid upon' Isaac the wood of sacrifice (Gen. 22:6), and at 23:33 'they came to the place' is the same expression as when Abraham and Isaac painfully 'came to the place'[5] of sacrifice (Gen. 22:9). The two allusions together are enough to suggest comparison of the two events by a reminiscence of this heart-rending scene of Abraham's obedience and trust.

Within this framework is another frame, again formed from a personal group, the women of Jerusalem. Following Jesus (and therefore included among his disciples) is the 'large number of the people and women' (23:27). Luke again uses the significant term λαός which specifically indicates the People of God, the chosen People. He has stressed continually that, though the leaders oppose Jesus, the people are favourably inclined towards him. But on this occasion it is the women who take centre-stage; Jesus turns to the women, addressing them as 'Daughters of Jerusalem'. The mourning of the women may be a fulfilment of Zechariah 12:10–14,

> They will mourn for the one whom they have pierced, as though for an only child, and weep for him as people weep for a first-born child. When that day comes, the mourning in Jerusalem will be as great as the mourning for Hadad Rimmon in the Plain of Megiddo. And the country will mourn clan by clan . . . and their women by themselves.

Jesus' words are full of prophetic solemnity and doom as he tells them to mourn for themselves, first with the threat of a Lukan beatitude (how characteristic this form is of Luke is shown by 1:45; 7:23; 11:27–28; 14:14–15, etc.), then with a prediction of the fulfilment of the threat in Hosea 10:8, and finally with the proverb about green wood and dry, alluding to the threat in Ezekiel 21:3. The increased significance of this passage comes, however, from its pairing both backwards and forwards. Backwards, at the end of Jesus' Jerusalem ministry, it pairs with his sorrowful threat as he wept over Jerusalem at the beginning of his ministry there (19:40–44), and so frames the Jerusalem ministry with Jesus' sorrow at their failure to respond. Forwards, it pairs with

---

[5] Characteristically Luke omits the Aramaic version of the name, Golgotha (itself a simplification of the unpronounceable 'Golgoltha'), as incomprehensible to his readers.

the final recognition of Jesus and repentance by the crowds and the 'women who had followed Jesus from Galilee' at his death (23:48–49). From this double-faced angle the short speech underlines two aspects, the impending doom of Jerusalem – and it must surely refer to the destruction which would come upon the city in AD 70 – and the repentance and welcome of Jesus' message by at least some of the Chosen People. In the course of the narrative this is again underlined (23:35): 'the People stood there looking on', contrasting with the rulers who mocked Jesus.

CHRISTOLOGICAL FOCUS

Luke avoids what he seems to consider duplications in the narrative, as he often does. There was only one account of the miraculous feeding (9:10–17) while Mark and Matthew have one feeding of 5,000 and another of 4,000. There was only one scene of Jesus calming the storm (8:22–25), whereas Mark and Matthew have both this and Jesus walking on the water, which Luke omitted probably as a doublet of the calming of the storm. Having related the story of the woman anointing Jesus' feet (7:38) Luke omitted the somewhat similar incident, given in all three other gospels, of anointing of Jesus' head at Bethany. So in the narrative of the crucifixion Luke omits the first offer of a drink to Jesus (Mark 15:23; Matt. 27:34), giving only an equivalent of the second offer, that of rough wine, and taking up the hint in Mark that it is an element in the mockery of the crucified Jesus (23:36). He also omits the earlier of the two cries of Jesus on the cross, the intonation of the Psalm (Mark 15:34; Matt. 27:46) and the consequent taunts about Elijah, recounting only the dying cry of Jesus, to which he gives – as we shall see – a special content. Luke alone attributes the mockery of Jesus on the cross to the soldiers (23:36), but does not have the mockery of Jesus by the soldiers in the praetorium (Mark 15:16–20); perhaps he is combining the two.

The remarkable change in the mockery on the cross is its focus. To begin with, the taunt about the Temple has disappeared completely, but then Luke's attitude towards the Temple is quite different from that of Mark and Matthew. For in this gospel Jesus cleanses, rather than rubbishes, the Temple, and then uses it as the locus for his own daily teaching and preaching. It will continue to be used and honoured by the early community in the Acts of the Apostles. The Lukan Jesus does not evince the hostility to the Temple which is mocked in the other synoptics, both at trial and at execution. In the Lukan trial before Pilate the accusations were sharply focused on two claims, Christ and King of the Jews (23:2–3). So now, appropriately, the mockery is again focused on the same two titles, 'the Christ of God, the Chosen One' (this last title being an allusion to the Song of the Servant in Isaiah and to the Lukan account of the Transfiguration, 9:35) and 'King of the Jews'. So, while in Mark and Matthew Jesus is crucified and mocked because of his action in the Temple, in Luke the concentration falls upon the messianic and royal claims.

Stronger, however, than either of these titles, and showing the meaning which they have for Luke, is the view of Jesus as Saviour. With heavy sarcasm 'Saviour' is attached to each of the titles with which he is taunted: 'He saved others, let him save himself if he is the Christ of God, the Chosen One' and 'If you are the King of the Jews, save yourself.' Throughout the gospel Luke has stressed that Jesus is the Saviour, in a way much clearer than Mark and Matthew. This may be for either of two reasons. In the hellenistic world there were plenty of Saviour-Gods, committal to and initiation into whose cults was held to guarantee protection and salvation from the uncertainties and disasters of that unpredictable age. Luke, writing for a hellenistic audience, confronts such beliefs head-on, with the claim that Jesus is the true Saviour-God. From the Hebrew point of view also it may be that Mark's and Matthew's Christology was not yet sufficiently advanced explicitly to call Jesus the Saviour, for this was traditionally a title of Yahweh. Apart from a single mention in John 4:42, Luke is the only evangelist to use the words 'Saviour' and 'salvation' of Jesus. This he does frequently, especially in the infancy narrative, where he is writing more freely ('a horn of salvation', 'salvation from our enemies', 'a Saviour who is Christ the Lord', 1:69, 71, 77; 2:11, 30; 3:6), and in the speeches of Acts ('leader and Saviour', 'salvation in none other', 'God gives them salvation through his hand', Acts 4:12; 5:31; 7:25; 13:23). The other gospels had frequently spoken of Jesus 'saving' through his healing miracles, but this saving takes on a quite new connotation through the stress on Jesus as Saviour. Now it is not merely physical healing that is implied but something deeper. It was a bold step in the development of Christology to apply to Jesus the divine attribute of

Saviour. The ironical stress on it in each mockery, even that of the unrepentant thief, means that it cannot be said that Luke attributes no salvific value to the death of Jesus.[6]

A SCENE OF REPENTANCE AND HEALING

Forgiveness, healing and repentance have been features of the whole of Luke's gospel (see p. 60), but come to their climax in the climax of the gospel. Even as Jesus is nailed to the cross he forgives his executioners.[7] Then he welcomes the good thief into his kingdom.[8] Finally the gentiles, represented by the centurion, give glory to God, and the Jews, represented by the crowd of onlookers, go home beating their breasts in repentance.

The transformation from the Markan scene of horror and suffering into this scene of salvation and triumph is completed by the transfer of two events and by Jesus' final cry. The mention of darkness over the earth (in Luke, frankly an eclipse) and the rending of the veil of the Temple are transferred by Luke to before the death of Jesus. This

---

[6] This assertion often seems to rest on Luke's omission of the Markan saying, 'The son of man came . . . to give his life as a ransom for many' (Mark 10:45).

[7] The manuscript evidence for the inclusion or exclusion of this verse is very evenly balanced. Was it omitted by anti-Jewish copyists in a period of controversy, as too favourable to the Jews? Or because the destruction of Jerusalem seemed to give it the lie? Bruce Metzger in his magisterial *Textual Commentary on the Greek New Testament* thinks that 'the logion, though probably not a part of the original Gospel of Luke, bears self-evident tokens of its dominical origin' (Metzger, 1994, p. 154). It could also be argued that the ἄφες . . . γὰρ and the unadorned πάτερ are Lukan characteristics (as 11:2, 4).

[8] This little scene is typical of Luke, and typical of the way he builds up a rich scene from a slight hint (Luke 12:17–19 from Ecclus. (Sir.) 11:18–20; Luke 14:1–6 from Proverbs 25:6–7; Luke 18:1–8 from Ecclus. (Sir.) 35:14–15). He takes the two criminals of Mark's account and makes them one of the contrasting pairs he so likes (Zechariah >< Mary, John the Baptist >< Jesus, the prodigal son >< his elder brother, Dives >< Lazarus, Martha >< Mary, the Pharisee >< the tax-collector). They break into dialogue, as so often in Luke's proper parables. The unadorned vocative, 'Ιησοῦ, unique in the gospels, is a typical Lukan touch of warmth. The first prerequisite for becoming a disciple is always admission of sinfulness (Peter in 5:8; the woman in 7:38; the tax-collector in 18:13). The vocabulary is also thoroughly Lukan, though Raymond Brown suggests, on the grounds of the 'Amen' and the un-Lukan 'paradise', that Luke has taken and re-positioned a traditional saying of Jesus by which he promised salvation to a repentant sinner (Brown, 1994, p. 1001).

enables Luke to bring the scene to a peaceful conclusion full of hope, confidence and salvation. Gone is the agonised final shriek, gone the shattering reaction signifying the vacuity of the Temple, gone Matthew's daunting apocalyptic cosmic turmoil. Jesus' final cry, instead of being what might seem, at any rate to Luke's hellenistic audience, to be a cry of despair, is transformed into a confident prayer of self-surrender, again – as Mark's 'My God, my God, why have you forsaken me?' – drawn from a psalm, namely Psalm 30:6. The emphasis is on the salvific obedience of Jesus, which Paul would see as reversing the disobedience of Adam, on the triple acknowledgement by centurion, bystanders and friends of Jesus, and on the welcome given to salvation by the repentance of the crowds.

JOHN'S ACCOUNT

In his noble adornment of the crucifixion scene John produces one of the finest pieces in his gospel, a fitting climax to his account of Jesus' triumphant Passion. It is a scene not of degrading torture but of ennobled triumph, presided over by Jesus and fulfilling the predictions, which have dominated the earlier outlook on the Passion, that it would be the hour of his exaltation and of his glorification (see pp. 24–26). From the point of view of John's Church, it is also the hour of the foundation of the Christian community.

JESUS REIGNS

The control of Jesus and his royalty are indicated in several ways. Negatively, the degrading elements are removed. There is no mockery by the Jewish authorities (as in Mark and Matthew) or by the soldiers (as in Luke), no cry of dereliction, no final shriek, no agony of thirst. Instead of Simon of Cyrene being press-ganged to carry the burden of the cross, Jesus himself hoists it voluntarily: βαστάζων ἑαυτῷ, 'hoisting for himself' (19:17), suggests almost that Jesus swings the cross willingly and easily onto his shoulder, setting off unaided and unguided on his own path. The actual crucifixion, again described only in a single word, seems to be mentioned solely in order to indicate that Jesus is placed in the middle between two others, as though they were his supporters or courtiers.

Major emphasis is placed upon the *titulus,* authoritatively written by Pilate himself, with the insistence, in the teeth of Jewish opposition, that Jesus really is the King of the Jews, not merely the claimant to be King. The authoritative nature of this public proclamation is increased by its being written (and seemingly by Pilate himself) not only in Hebrew, but in the two major world-languages, Greek and Latin. A certain degree of respect or even reverence is shown by the care of the soldiers not to divide Jesus' main garment, his χιτών, woven in one piece throughout. Whether John intended further symbolism, suggesting the High Priestly robe (a single weave according to Josephus, *Antiquities,* 3.161) or the unbroken unity of the Church, remains entirely unclear.

Jesus' control continues throughout the scene. He has the freedom to see and commend to each other his mother and the beloved disciple (about which more later). Then, as the final climax approaches, the reader is again reminded of Jesus' foreknowledge by that keyword εἰδώς, 'knowing'. This is an echo of that self-possessed knowledge which has marked the Johannine Jesus at key moments of the Passion Narrative. It is noted twice in quick succession at the preparatory moment of the Supper: 'Jesus, knowing that his hour had come to pass from this world to the Father', 'Jesus, knowing that the Father had put everything into his hands' (13:1, 3), and again, resumptively, at the beginning of the arrest – for John the beginning of the Narrative proper – 'Jesus, knowing everything that was to happen to him' (18:4). Now, one more time the reader is reminded of his control, 'Jesus, knowing that everything was completed' (19:28). Finally, only when Jesus has himself noted that all is completed, and has bowed his head in readiness and acquiescence, does he (again a positive action on his part, rather than something he undergoes) breathe forth his spirit.

THE FOUNDATION OF THE CHURCH

There have often been hints, throughout the gospel, of the sacraments of baptism and the eucharist, particularly in the prominence of 'living water' or 'the water of life' in the dialogues with the Samaritan and with Nicodemus (especially 4:10, 11; and 7:38), and in the bread of life discourse (6:31–66). Equally significant, however, is the lack of a narrative of the institution of the eucharist at the Last Supper. John is not ready for the sacraments to be founded. This, however, changes

with the remarkable event which immediately precedes the note that
Jesus knew that now everything had been completed. This is the scene
of which the synoptics have no glimmering, the commendation of Jesus'
mother and the beloved disciple to each other.

Each of these two has an important representative role. Whether the
beloved disciple was or was not originally a particular person has been
endlessly debated.[9] Much more significant is the fact that this gospel
deliberately leaves him faceless. He features at four climactic moments.
He is close to Jesus at the Last Supper, reclining next to Jesus (13:23)
in intimacy of union. He shares with Jesus in the Passion by his
presence here at the foot of the cross. He runs with Peter to the empty
tomb, yields precedence of entry to Peter, but contrasts with Peter by
achieving understanding and faith (20:8). Lastly, the beloved disciple
features in the appendix, 21:20–24, as the guarantor of the gospel
tradition, who is to remain until the Lord comes. This is a complete
sketch of the generic disciple whom Jesus loves, the disciple who is
close to Jesus at the eucharist, who shares the Passion with Jesus, who
recognises and believes in the Resurrection, and who is therefore the
enduring tradent and surety of the gospel tradition until the Lord
comes. This being the meaning and task of every beloved disciple, it
is necessary that the face should be left empty, to be filled by the
features of every true disciple.

Similarly with the mother of Jesus, who is never named in this
gospel, either here or in the Marriage-Feast at Cana, which surely looks
to and anticipates this account. There her part was to share in Jesus'
miracle, indeed to occasion it despite Jesus' initial reluctance. The
mysterious mention of the hour (2:4) linked that early scene to this
climactic moment of the hour of Jesus. The strange appellation γύναι
(whose rendering as 'Woman!' is too bluff, and as 'Lady!' too courtly)
is not elsewhere used of a son to his mother, but also links 2:4 to
19:26. This mode of address imparts a certain impersonality to the
scene, as though the archetypal mother is now being joined to
the archetypal male disciple. The importance of these two archetypal
disciples being entrusted to each other has been seen as exemplifying
Jesus' care for his mother: he arranges a home for her, put into practice

---

[9] The traditional identification with John, son of Zebedee, is no better founded than
the more modern identification with Lazarus.

according to the legend by John taking her to the Holy House at
Ephesus. To limit the message to such material care would be not only
one-sided but also superficial. The real importance of the final dying
action of Jesus is the formation of a new relationship. They form the
first faithful community of the followers of Jesus, the mother who first
set Jesus on the road to his hour, and the beloved disciple, the ideal of
all disciples.

This formation of the first Christian community is immediately followed by two other ecclesiastically significant events. The evangelist
next tells the reader that Jesus knew that everything was complete.
Jesus' own last word is the same, τετέλεσται, after which he bows his
head and yields up his spirit, παρέδωκεν τὸ πνεῦμα, literally 'handed
over the spirit'. The verb τελειόω has frequently been used by Jesus
of completing the Father's will: he says to the Samaritan, 'My food is
to do the will of the one who sent me and to complete his work' (4:34,
cf. 5:36; 17:4). In view of the frequency of Johannine double layers of
meaning ('living water', 'lifted up from the earth') this handing over
must be seen to conceal a deeper layer of meaning, that Jesus handed
over his Spirit to give life to his community. John's gospel is studded
with paradoxes and contrasts. This would be the reverse of the same
paradox as occurred in the raising of Lazarus: Jesus' gift of life to
Lazarus was the event which finally pushed the Jewish authorities
to determine on Jesus' death. So now in reverse it is the death of Jesus
which gives life to his community, the coming of the Spirit of
Jesus which was promised in the last discourses (14:16–17, 25–26;
15:26; 16:13), and is again exemplified in Jesus breathing on the
disciples in the upper room on the evening of Easter Sunday (20:22).

The second significant event follows when the soldier pierces Jesus'
side. This event has double significance, biblical and ecclesiastical.
Firstly, John explains that the abstention of the soldiers from breaking
Jesus' legs fulfils the scripture of the Paschal lamb, 'Not a bone of his
shall be broken' (Exod. 12:46; John 19:36). There have been hints that
Jesus takes the place of the Paschal lamb ever since John the Baptist
pointed Jesus out as the Lamb of God (1:29, 36). There the meaning
of this title remained unclear, but during the Passion there have been
clearer hints. John points out (19:14) that it was the Day of Preparation
for the Passover, and Jesus dies at the same time as the Paschal lambs
were being slaughtered in the Temple in preparation for the festal

meal.[10] This may also be the sense of the strange statement that the sponge offered to Jesus to quench his thirst was on a hyssop-branch (19:29). Hyssop is a springy little plant, whose leafy little stems seldom exceed a few centimetres.[11] No way could any sponge be fastened to it, nor could it be used to extend the reach of the soldier offering the drink. This difficulty is no doubt the origin of the textual variant which gives υσσω for νσσωπω, that is 'lance' for 'hyssop', since a sponge on the end of a lance makes much more sense (as the frequency of this motif in artistic representations of the crucifixion attests). On the other hand the mention of hyssop at the crucifixion would make sense as an allusion to the instructions for the sprinkling with a sprig of hyssop of the blood of the Paschal lamb on the doorposts (Exod. 12:22).

The piercing of Jesus' side also gives a symbolism for the life of the Church, the life of the community flowing from the death of Jesus. This was focused by Christian writers onto the sacraments of baptism and eucharist at an early stage. The actual physical or medical phenomena are of little interest to the evangelist; it is doubtful whether he envisaged the exact medical processes involved. The point of the blood and water is their symbolic value. The association of water with Jesus' gift of life is obvious enough, and clearly envisaged by John. An important background to this is the conversation with the Samaritan in John 4:14, and the claim of John 7:38. In these passages Jesus is shown to be the source of living water or the water of life: 'No one who drinks the water that I shall give him will ever be thirsty again; the water that I shall give him will become in him a spring of water welling up for eternal life'. This in turn has as its background the river

---

[10] The symbolism of the simultaneity of the death of Jesus and of the Paschal lambs makes a major dislocation of dating: if Jesus died on the Day of Preparation, the Last Supper must have occurred on the previous day, rather than at the time normal for the Paschal meal. Three solutions have been proposed to this problem: (1) the Last Supper was not in fact a Paschal meal, (2) either John or the synoptic gospels allowed theology to overrule chronology and adjusted the dating to suit their theological purpose, or (3) Jesus used a different calendar, that in use at Qumran, by which the Passover supper was celebrated on a Wednesday evening. This original solution was strongly advocated by Jaubert, 1957.

[11] 1 Kings 4:33 expresses the breadth of Solomon's knowledge by saying, 'He could discourse on plants from the cedar in Lebanon to the hyssop growing on the wall'. Here hyssop is presented as the extreme opposite of the noble cedar, a mere excrescence from a crack between the stones.

of living water flowing from the Temple in Ezekiel 47:1–12.[12] This is more specifically and quasi-physically attached to Jesus as the new Temple in 7:37–8, when Jesus cries out in the Temple on the last day of the festival associated with living water, 'Let anyone who is thirsty come to me. Let anyone who believes in me come and drink', directing his hearers away from the building of the Temple to himself. Immediately afterwards John interprets this living water as the gift of the Spirit, in a way which specifically attaches it to the scene of the glorification at the hour of Jesus, 'He was speaking of the Spirit which those who believed in him were to receive, for there was no Spirit as yet because Jesus had not yet been glorified' (7:39). The water flowing from the side of Jesus is therefore an alternative symbolism, like the spirit handed over, of the outpouring of the Spirit at Jesus' death.

The flow of blood is more obscure. It may be one more allusion to the sacrifice of the Paschal lamb, connected with the requirement of Judaism in the Mishnah (*Pesahim*, 5.3) that the blood of the victim should flow (Brown, 1971, p. 951). Alternatively, it has been suggested that it is an anti-Docetic proof that Jesus was truly human – if indeed Docetism was a danger to which John wished to reply.

Christian tradition at a very early stage extended or focused the symbolism of water and blood on the sacraments of baptism and eucharist. While symbolism is difficult to exclude from the gospel of John at any level it remains questionable whether there is anything in the scene of the crucifixion which would constitute a direct allusion to the conversation with Nicodemus about being born again by water and the Spirit (3:5–8). It may be fair, therefore, to speak of an application rather than a direct allusion. Similarly with the blood and the eucharist – apart from one use of the term in 1:13, all the other references in John to blood are to the blood of Jesus in the eucharistic discourse (6:53–56). This does not, however, mean that any allusion in John to the blood of Jesus carries this sense.

---

[12] This marvellous passage can be fully appreciated only by those who can envisage standing on the eastern parapet of the Temple and looking out over the arid country towards the Dead Sea. Without some such miracle there is no chance of this barren heat-hazed landscape 'bearing new fruit every month', nor of the sulphur-smelling 'Asphalt Lake' becoming wholesome and teeming with fish.

ENDNOTE

It would be foolish and frustrating to finish without pulling together some of the strands of this investigation. There can, unfortunately, be no question of a full treatment of the conclusions which might be drawn. I can attempt no more than a personal interpretation, which is not, I hope, without foundation in the texts themselves. I wish to focus on two points, the historicity of the narrative and the sense of Jesus' death on the cross.

It will be clear that the evangelists are constantly interpreting, each in his own way and with relation to the aspects which he sees to be important. Whence did they derive their basic, factual information? Matthew and Luke certainly base their narratives on Mark. There is no strong evidence to show that they had any other factual, or at least any other written, source, for the treatment by each is characteristic of the methods and serves the purposes of each of these two evangelists. For example, there is no good reason to believe that Matthew had any factual information which lay behind his description of Pilate's wife's dream or of Pilate washing his hands, or that Luke had any factual information which lay behind the repentance of the good thief or Jesus' last words. Behind these two, Mark, and independently of all three, John, construct each his own narrative in accordance with the methods, style and interests which are evident from the rest of these two gospels. Mark's account of the agony in the garden makes sense in terms of his own interests and style, probably drawing on reflections of the early Christian community which can also be seen in the Letter to the Hebrews. Similarly there is no good reason to believe that John had any factual information which lay behind his version of the scene in

Pilate's praetorium, or behind the scene with Mary and the beloved disciple at the foot of the Cross.

At the other extreme we have the sound, traditional information given in 1 Corinthians 15:3, that 'Christ died for our sins in accordance with the scriptures', backed up by the non-biblical sources which consistently hold Pilate to be responsible for his execution. In many cases we can see how this fulfilment of the scriptures has been knitted into the narrative and prescribed some of the quasi-factual details, such as Matthew's addition of 'bile' to the drink offered to Jesus on the cross, or John's 'Not one bone of his shall be broken.' In other cases we have no means now of knowing whether the allusion gave rise to the fact or the fact gave rise to the allusion. Did Mark have information that Jesus was silent to his questioners and that two malefactors were crucified with him, or did he deduce that Jesus *must have been* silent because he was the Servant of the Lord, and that he *must have been* 'numbered among evil-doers' in fulfilment of the scriptures? Such details have value even today as powerful reminders respectively that Jesus – as we know from earlier passages of the gospel – saw himself as the Servant of the Lord, and providing the basis for Luke's sublime presentation of Jesus' act of forgiveness. More powerful still, they form together the expression, in the manner of first-century exegesis, of the fact that the crucifixion brings to a climax the long process of the revelation of God's love in the scriptures of Israel. In the twenty-first century we see God's work in Jesus at the crucifixion as the culmination of the long sweep of Israel's history, the promises of God to Abraham, to Moses and to David, the guidance of the Law, the progressively deepening appreciation of God's outgoing love in the face of human stubbornness. In the first century, as the scriptural exegesis of Qumran makes clear, such understanding was expressed through a whole series of little 'hooks' onto the scriptures of Judaism.

Between these two extremes there is a host of details which must have developed in the course of the oral transmission of the material in the Christian communities. How much was this development affected by their needs, crises and experiences? Throughout the gospels of Matthew and John the undertone of conflict with contemporary Judaism indicates that they express and emerge from a situation of conflict between Jewish groups who accepted Jesus as Messiah and Jewish groups who did not. It is no coincidence that these two gospels especially stress that Pilate was egged on by Jewish pressure to authorise the execution. The part of the Jewish authorities in achieving the execution does not feature in Paul's traditional summary nor in the skeletal non-biblical reports, though it is touched upon by Josephus' phrase 'at the suggestion of the principal men amongst us'. Matthew underlines this aspect by the notorious cry, 'His blood be upon us and upon our children.' John shows the full horror of the betrayal of Judaism in the trial-scene before Pilate, when the Jewish leaders abjure the central tenet of Judaism before Jesus the king and judge. This emphasis is not absent from Mark, although he is writing for a gentile audience; but, beset by the problems of failure under persecution, Mark pays far more attention to the failure of the disciples to stick with their Master. Luke, again, concerned that his sophisticated gentile audience should change their way of life, underlines repentance and the welcome given to the repentant sinner by the dying Saviour. Thus each of the gospels has its own undercurrents. How much of this flows from the evangelist's personal understanding of Christ, how much from the gradual polishing of stories re-told in the Christian communities, and how much from factual reportage of the actual events?

The other point to be touched is the sense of Jesus' death on the cross. Here I take my clue from the final union of Father and Son expressed in each of the gospels. Mark and Matthew show Jesus intoning Psalm 22, 'My God, my God, why have you forsaken me?' The meaning of this intonation comes from the psalm as a whole. Far from expressing any sense of Jesus' abandonment by God (as ignorance of the scriptures might suggest), the psalm concludes with the triumph of God and the vindication of the sufferer. With Jesus' dying commendation of himself to God, 'Into your hands I commend my spirit', Luke again expresses the union of Jesus with God. The same is the meaning of the final proclamation in John, τετέλεσται, 'It is fulfilled.' The whole impetus of Jesus' life and ministry had been the renewal of God's kingship by his teaching and the evidence of God's work wrought by his healing hands. Despite rejection by his people as a whole, despite incomprehension by his chosen Twelve, Jesus continued to proclaim this renewal of God's rule even in the Temple itself, despite the inevitable wrath of the authorities ruling Judaism. Obedience to his Father's command was thus the motive force which brought him to the cross. The moment of his utter self-denial in pursuance of his mission is the moment of perfect union of purpose between Father and Son.

Paul sees this obedience of the Second Adam as undoing the disobedience of Adam.

> One man's offence brought condemnation on all humanity. Just as by one man's disobedience many were made sinners, so by one man's obedience are many to be made upright (Rom. 5:18).

The story of Adam and Eve in the Garden is the myth, the analysis in pictorial form, of human disobedience, cause of disharmony and mistrust, fear and failure, plainly visible in every age of human history and literature, perhaps intensified as the social and scientific means of oppression have become refined. Unaided human beings had no power to escape from this deathly spiral. To break out of the nightmare an obedience greater than that achievable by human beings was required.

More than this, Jesus achieved this greater obedience as the icon of God, the expression of the divinity in human form. Only this could complete the communion of human nature with divine, expressed most fully on the cross. It also shows in human form the love of God for creatures, accepting the ultimate self-sacrifice to restore human nature to its intended purpose and freedom, justifying the many-layered meaning of the centurion's cry, 'In truth this man was son of God.'

BIBLIOGRAPHY

Ashton, John, *Understanding the Fourth Gospel* (Clarendon Press, 1991)

Bird, C. H., 'Some γάǫ-clauses in St Mark's Gospel', *Journal of Theological Studies* 4 (1953), 171–87

Bond, Helen K., 'The coins of Pontius Pilate: part of an attempt to provoke the people or to integrate them into the empire?', *Journal for the Study of Judaism* 27 (1996), 241–62

Bond, Helen K., *Pontius Pilate in History and Interpretation* (Cambridge University Press, 1998)

Brandon, S. G. F., *Jesus and the Zealots* (Manchester University Press, 1967)

Brown, Raymond E., *Introduction to the New Testament* (Doubleday, 1996)

Brown, Raymond E., *The Death of the Messiah* (Geoffrey Chapman, 1994)

Brown, Raymond E., *The Gospel According to John* (Geoffrey Chapman, 1971)

Bultmann, Rudolf, *Glauben und Verstehen* (Mohr, Tübingen, 1961)

Bultmann, Rudolf, *New Testament Theology* (SCM Press, 1974)

Burkitt, F. C., *The Gospel History and its Transmission* (T. & T. Clark, 1906)

Burridge, Richard, *What Are the Gospels?* (Cambridge University Press, 1992)

Cathcart, Kevin, *The Targum of the Minor Prophets* (Michael Glazier, 1989)

Crossan, John Dominic, *The Historical Jesus, the Life of a Mediterranean Jewish Peasant* (T. & T. Clark, 1991)

Dierx, W, and Garbrecht, G (ed.), *Wasser im heiligen Land* (von Zabern, 2001)

Donnelly, Doris (ed.), *Jesus, a Colloquium in the Holy Land* (Continuum, 2001)

Downing, F. Gerald, *Christ and the Cynics* (JSOT Manuals, 4, Sheffield Academic Press, 1988)

Ehrenberg, V., and Jones, A. H. M., *Documents Illustrating the Reigns of Augustus and Tiberius* (Clarendon Press, 1955)

Elliott, J. K., *The Language and Style of the Gospel of Mark* (Brill, 1993)

Fitzmyer, J., 'Abba and Jesus' Relation to God' in *A cause de l'évangile*, ed. F. Refoulé (Le Cerf, 1985)

Freedman, David Noel (ed.), *Anchor Bible Dictionary* (Doubleday, 1992)

Goodman, M., *The Ruling Class of Judaea* (Cambridge University Press, 1987)

Goulder, Michael D., *Midrash and Lection in Matthew* (SPCK, 1974)

Green, H. Benedict, *Matthew, Poet of the Beatitudes* (Sheffield Academic Press, 2001)

Hill, Sir G. F., *Catalogue of the Greek coins of Palestine: Galilee, Samaria and Judaea* (London, 1914)

Holleran, J. Warren, *The Synoptic Gethsemane* (Universita Gregoriana, 1973)

Jaubert, Annie, *La date de la Cène* (Gabalda, 1957)

Jeremias, Joachim, *The Central Message of the New Testament* (SCM Press, 1965)

Johnson, Luke Timothy, *The Real Jesus* (HarperSanFrancisco, 1996)

Lintott, A., *Imperium Romanum* (Routledge, 1993)

Longenecker, Richard N., *Biblical Exegesis in the Apostolic Period* (Eerdmans, 1975)

Lüdemann, Gerd, *Jesus After 2000 Years, What He Really Said and Did* (SCM Press, 2000)

Matera, F. J., 'Jesus before Annas' in *Ephemerides Theologicae Lovanienses* 66 (1990),

Matera, F. J., 'Luke 23:1–15', 'Luke 22:66–71' in F. Neirynck, *L'évangile de Luc* (Leuven University Press, 1989)

McGing, B. C., 'Pontius Pilate and the Sources' in *Catholic Bibilical Quarterly* 53 (1991) 416–38

McLaren, James S., *Power and Politics in Palestine* (Sheffield Academic Press, 1991)

Metzger, Bruce, *Textual Commentary on the Greek New Testament* (United Bible Societies, 1994)

Neill, Stephen and Wright, N. T., *The Interpretation of the New Testament, 1861–1986* (Oxford University Press, 1988)

Neirynck, F., *Duality in Mark* (Leuven University Press, 1988)

Nodet, Etienne, *Le Fils de Dieu* (Le Cerf, 2002)

Perrin, Norman, *Rediscovering the Teaching of Jesus* (SCM Press, 1967)

Porter, Stanley E., *The Criteria for Authenticity in Historical-Jesus Research* (Sheffield Academic Press, 2000)

Puéch, E., '4Q425 et la pericope des Béatitudes en Ben-Sira et Matthieu' in *Revue biblique 98* (1991)

Sanders, E. P., *Jesus and Judaism* (SCM Press, 1985)

Sanders, E. P., *Judaism, Practice and Belief, 63 BCE – 66 CE* (SCM Press, 1992)

Sanders, E. P., *The Historical Figure of Jesus* (Allen Lane, 1993)

Schürer, E., *The History of the Jewish People in the Age of Jesus Christ*, revised and edited by Geza Vermes and Fergus Millar (T. & T. Clark, 1973)

Schweitzer, Albert, *The Quest of the Historical Jesus* (1906; English: SCM Press, 1981)

Senior, Donald P., *The Passion Narrative according to Matthew* (Leuven University Press, 1975)

Shellard, B., 'The Relationship of Luke and John, a fresh look at an old problem' in *Journal of Theological Studies* 46 (1995) 71–98

Sherwin-White, A. N., *Roman Society and Roman Law in the New Testament* (Clarendon Press, 1963)

Van der Horst. P. W., 'The Birkat ha-minim in Recent Research' in *Expository Times* 105 (1994) 365–8.

Vanhoye, Albert, 'Les Récits de la Passion chez les Synoptiques' in *Nouvelle Revue Théologique* 89 (1967) 135–163

Vermes, G., *The Changing Faces of Jesus* (Allen Lane, 2000)

Vermes, G., *Jesus the Jew* (Collins, 1973)

Vivano, B., 'The High Priest's Servant's Ear' in *Revue biblique* 96 (1989) 71–80

Von Wahlde, U., *The Earliest Version of John's Gospel* (Wilmington, Michael Glazier, 1989)

Walaskay, Paul W., *'And so we came to Rome'* (Cambridge University Press, 1983)

Wansbrough, Henry, 'Suffered under Pontius Pilate' in *Scripture* 18 (1966) 84–93

Weeden, Theodore, 'The Heresy that Necessitated Mark's Gospel' in *Zeitschrift für neutestamentliche Wissenschaft* 59 (1968) 145–58

Wrede, William, *The Messianic Secret in the Gospels* (1901, English: Attic Press, 1971)

Wright, N. T., *Who was Jesus?* (SPCK, 1992)

SCRIPTURAL INDEX

Gen. 9:6 60
Gen. 22:5 52
Gen. 22:6 113
Gen. 22:9 113
Gen. 24:3 76
Gen. 29:32–35 65

Ex. 3:14 65
Ex. 10:22 110
Ex. 12:22 121
Ex. 12:46 120

Lev. 21:18 58

Deut. 21:6 88

Judg. 21:7 76

1 Sam. 4:21–22 65

2 Sam. 7:4 88
2 Sam. 7:10 70
2 Sam. 17:23 87

1 Kings 4:33 121

2 Kings 4:42–44 4

Job 1:9 73

Ps. 22 105, 106, 110, 125
Ps. 22:1 51
Ps. 22:7 51
Ps. 22:18 51, 103
Ps. 22:27–31 106
Ps. 23:2 4
Ps. 27:12 72
Ps. 30:6 117
Ps. 35:11 51, 72
Ps. 36:9 65
Ps. 38:11 52
Ps. 42:5 51
Ps. 69:21 102
Ps. 69:21a 109
Ps. 69:21b 103
Ps. 82:6 73
Ps. 110 26
Ps. 110:1 73
Ps. 116:1–8 48
Ps. 117 5

Ps. 118 5, 79

Prov. 25:6–7 116

Isa. 14:5 69
Isa. 42:1 18
Isa. 43:10–11 65
Isa. 45:18–19 82
Isa. 50:6 51, 74
Isa. 51:17 52
Isa. 53 85
Isa. 53:7 26, 51, 72
Isa. 53:12 52, 103
Isa. 54:1 69

Jer. 4:23–24 111
Jer. 25:15–16 52
Jer. 26:15 91
Jer. 39:8–15 87

Ezek. 1 74
Ezek. 21:3 113
Ezek. 32:7–8 105
Ezek. 34 65
Ezek. 37:12–13 111
Ezek. 47:1–12 122

Dan. 2:46 66
Dan. 7:13 73

Hos. 10:8 113
Hos. 11:1 73

Joel 2:10 105, 111

Amos 2:16 51
Amos 5:18 52
Amos 5:20 105
Amos 8:9 105

Zech. 11:12–13 87
Zech. 11:3 88
Zech. 12:10–14 113
Zech. 13:7 51, 58
Zech. 14:4 111

Mal. 3:1 106

Tob. 13:16–17 69

Wisd. 2:17–20 110

Wisd. 2:18 73
Wisd. 7:26 65

Ecclus. (Sir.) 11:18–20 116
Ecclus. (Sir.) 23:1 52
Ecclus. (Sir.) 35:14–15 116
Ecclus. (Sir.) 37:2 59

2 Macc. 3:16 56
2 Macc. 15:19 56

4 Macc. 6:6, 11 56

Matt. 1:20 88
Matt. 1:23 54
Matt. 2:13, 19 88
Matt. 2:16–18 20
Matt. 3:14–15 10
Matt. 4:3, 6 109
Matt. 4:12–16 91
Matt. 5:1 59
Matt. 5:10 20
Matt. 5:11 20
Matt. 5:32 3
Matt. 5:34 76
Matt. 5—7 5
Matt. 6:9 54
Matt. 6:10 21, 54
Matt. 8—9 5
Matt. 8:5–13 4, 91
Matt. 8:22 10, 60
Matt. 9:8 54
Matt. 9:35—10:16 13
Matt. 10:16–31 21
Matt. 10:17 21, 36
Matt. 10:33 76
Matt. 10:34–35 21
Matt. 10:40 60
Matt. 11:2–15 71
Matt. 12:6 75
Matt. 12:37 60
Matt. 14:30 77
Matt. 15:21–28 4
Matt. 16:16 76
Matt. 18:18 54
Matt. 18:20 54
Matt. 18:26 62

Matt. 20:13 59
Matt. 21:8–9 4
Matt. 21:28–32 91
Matt. 21:43 91
Matt. 22:9 61
Matt. 22:12 59
Matt. 23:1–36 21
Matt. 23:16–22 98
Matt. 24 21
Matt. 24:3 88
Matt. 24:20 21
Matt. 26:2 76
Matt. 26:14 58
Matt. 26:20–25 57
Matt. 26:22–23 57
Matt. 26:36–46 53
Matt. 26:38, 40 54
Matt. 26:39 53
Matt. 26:39, 42 54
Matt. 26:40 54
Matt. 26:40, 45 54
Matt. 26:42 54
Matt. 26:44 54
Matt. 26:47–56 59
Matt. 26:51 58
Matt. 26:56 60
Matt. 26:57–75 75
Matt. 26:58 75
Matt. 26:59 36
Matt. 26:63 109
Matt. 26:69 76
Matt. 26:75 76
Matt. 27:1–31 87
Matt. 27:3–10 51
Matt. 27:6 87
Matt. 27:9–10 60
Matt. 27:13–14 89
Matt. 27:15 90
Matt. 27:16 89
Matt. 27:17 89, 90
Matt. 27:20 90, 91
Matt. 27:21 90
Matt. 27:22 90
Matt. 27:23 90
Matt. 27:24 88
Matt. 27:25 90
Matt. 27:34 114
Matt. 27:40 109
Matt. 27:42 110
Matt. 27:45 110
Matt. 27:46 114
Matt. 27:49 110
Matt. 27:51b–52 111
Matt. 27:53 111
Matt. 27:62 71
Matt. 28:16–20 91
Matt. 28:18–20 54

Mark 1:1 73
Mark 1:11 73, 107
Mark 1:13 56
Mark 1:15 48

Mark 1:16–20 49
Mark 1:21—2:1 5
Mark 1:24 73
Mark 1:25 72
Mark 1:44 72
Mark 2:1–12 18
Mark 2:1—3:6 5, 18, 79
Mark 2:17 14
Mark 2:20 18
Mark 2:23–28 70
Mark 2:5–10 71
Mark 3:1–6 70
Mark 3:6 18
Mark 3:12 72
Mark 3:13–15 49
Mark 3:13–35 18
Mark 3:21–26 9
Mark 3:22 71
Mark 4:1–34 79
Mark 4:11 49
Mark 4:13 49
Mark 4:38–40 49
Mark 5:7 73
Mark 5:21–43 61
Mark 6:1–6 5
Mark 6:7–11 13
Mark 6:12–13 49
Mark 6:29 19
Mark 6:30–31 49
Mark 6:30–44 3, 4
Mark 6:37 49
Mark 6:39 4
Mark 6:50 65
Mark 7:14–23 70
Mark 7:18 49
Mark 7:24–30 4, 11, 108
Mark 7:36 72
Mark 8:1–10 3
Mark 8:17 49
Mark 8:19–20 4
Mark 8:22–26 5
Mark 8:29 49, 72, 107
Mark 8:31 19
Mark 8:31–38 72
Mark 8:32 49
Mark 8:34 19
Mark 8:38 73
Mark 9:6 48
Mark 9:7 73
Mark 9:9 19, 72, 108
Mark 9:31 19
Mark 9:31–37 72
Mark 9:32 50
Mark 9:35 19
Mark 10:1–12 70
Mark 10:11–12 3
Mark 10:32–34 19
Mark 10:32–45 72
Mark 10:35 50
Mark 10:37 104
Mark 10:38–39 52

Mark 10:39 19, 50
Mark 10:45 116
Mark 10:46–52 5
Mark 11:8–9 4, 5
Mark 11:12 79
Mark 11:12–21 69
Mark 11:13–20 18
Mark 11:20 79
Mark 11:28 92
Mark 12:1–37 5
Mark 12:13 71
Mark 12:13–37 79
Mark 13 21
Mark 13:2 69
Mark 13:9 19, 36
Mark 13:11 48
Mark 13:26 73
Mark 13:32 48
Mark 13:33, 34, 35, 37 48
Mark 14:1 71, 79
Mark 14:10, 20, 43 58
Mark 14:12 79
Mark 14:17–21 57
Mark 14:18 57
Mark 14:23–24 52
Mark 14:27 59
Mark 14:31, 50 50
Mark 14:32–43 46
Mark 14:34 52
Mark 14:35 48, 52
Mark 14:36 54
Mark 14:37 54
Mark 14:37, 38 49
Mark 14:39 48, 54
Mark 14:40 48, 54
Mark 14:42 48
Mark 14:43 71
Mark 14:43–52 57
Mark 14:53 68, 71, 85
Mark 14:53–72 69
Mark 14:54 68, 69
Mark 14:55 36
Mark 14:58, 69, 72 69
Mark 14:58, 72 69
Mark 14:59 75
Mark 14:60 85
Mark 14:60, 61 68
Mark 14:61 85
Mark 14:61, 68, 71 68
Mark 14:61, 70 69
Mark 14:62 85
Mark 14:63 76
Mark 14:63, 64 68
Mark 14:64 69
Mark 14:65 76, 85
Mark 14:65, 69, 71 69
Mark 14:66–68 68
Mark 14:68 68
Mark 14:69 75
Mark 15:1 36, 71, 85
Mark 15:2 85, 92

Mark 15:2, 4 84
Mark 15:2–5 84
Mark 15:2, 9, 12, 18, 26 85
Mark 15:2–20 84
Mark 15:3 84, 96
Mark 15:3–5 85
Mark 15:4 72, 84, 85, 96
Mark 15:4, 5 85
Mark 15:5 85
Mark 15:6–15 86
Mark 15:7 86, 89
Mark 15:8 86
Mark 15:10 86, 90
Mark 15:12, 13 86
Mark 15:13, 14 90
Mark 15:16–20 85, 96, 114
Mark 15:21 102
Mark 15:22–27 102
Mark 15:23 114
Mark 15:23, 36 102
Mark 15:24, 25 102
Mark 15:25, 33, 34 5
Mark 15:25, 33, 34, 42 79
Mark 15:26 100
Mark 15:28 104
Mark 15:29 69
Mark 15:29–32 102
Mark 15:31 71
Mark 15:33–37 102
Mark 15:34 52, 114
Mark 15:34, 37 102
Mark 15:38–41 102
Mark 15:39 72
Mark 15:40–41 102
Mark 15:45–46 19
Mark 16:7 76

Luke 1:32 78
Luke 1:45 113
Luke 1:69, 71, 77 115
Luke 2:11, 30 115
Luke 2:35 22
Luke 2:52 64
Luke 3:6 115
Luke 4:13 22, 62
Luke 4:16–30 5, 22
Luke 4:27 61
Luke 4:41 78
Luke 5:1–11 4, 60
Luke 5:8 116
Luke 7:1–10 4, 60
Luke 7:11–17 61
Luke 7:23 113
Luke 7:36–50 61
Luke 7:38 114, 116
Luke 7:38, 44 61
Luke 7:42 62
Luke 8:22–25 114
Luke 8:40–56 61
Luke 9:9 95
Luke 9:10–17 114
Luke 9:31 23

Luke 9:35 115
Luke 9:41 93
Luke 9:51 23
Luke 9:51—18:14 22
Luke 11:2, 4 116
Luke 11:27–28 113
Luke 12:17–19 116
Luke 12:49–50 23
Luke 13:31 96
Luke 13:33 22
Luke 13:34 23
Luke 13:6–9 61
Luke 14:1–6 116
Luke 14:14–15 113
Luke 14:21, 23 61
Luke 15:8–32 61
Luke 18:1–8 116
Luke 18:13 116
Luke 19:3–5 61
Luke 19:40–44 113
Luke 19:45–46 78
Luke 19:47 23, 78, 92
Luke 19:48 23
Luke 20:1–2 92
Luke 20:20–26 93
Luke 21:12 95
Luke 21:37 23, 92
Luke 22:3 22
Luke 22:15–16 23
Luke 22:21–38 61
Luke 22:36–38 58
Luke 22:40–46 55
Luke 22:43 48
Luke 22:43–44 55
Luke 22:45 55, 61
Luke 22:45, 46 55
Luke 22:47–53 60
Luke 22:50 61
Luke 22:51 55
Luke 22:52 62
Luke 22:53 55
Luke 22:54–71 77
Luke 22:61 77
Luke 22:66 36, 94
Luke 22:66–67 61
Luke 22:67 82
Luke 23:1–25 92
Luke 23:2 93
Luke 23:2–3 92, 115
Luke 23:4 94, 95
Luke 23:4, 14, 22 61
Luke 23:5 93, 94
Luke 23:8 95
Luke 23:9 72, 96
Luke 23:10 96
Luke 23:11 93, 96
Luke 23:12 96
Luke 23:13 95
Luke 23:14 93, 94
Luke 23:18 94, 95
Luke 23:21 94

Luke 23:22 94
Luke 23:23 94
Luke 23:24 94
Luke 23:26 55, 112
Luke 23:27 113
Luke 23:33 113
Luke 23:35 114
Luke 23:36 114
Luke 23:46 52, 55
Luke 23:48–49 114
Luke 23:49 62, 112
Luke 24:10 61
Luke 24:12 61
Luke 24:26, 39, 40 61
Luke 24:41 55, 61
Luke 24:50–53 61

John 1:11–12 98
John 1:13 122
John 1:29, 36 120
John 1:35–50 97
John 1:38 66
John 1:46 101
John 1:48–50 63
John 1:50 97
John 2:4 24, 47, 119
John 2:19 26, 69
John 2:25 63
John 3:3 99
John 3:3–6 25
John 3:3, 5 96
John 3:5–8 122
John 3:6 98
John 3:10 101
John 3:10–21 3
John 3:14 26
John 3:19 98
John 4:10, 11 118
John 4:10–15 99
John 4:12 100
John 4:14 121
John 4:21, 23 24
John 4:34 120
John 4:42 115
John 4:46–53 4, 60
John 5:18 27
John 5:19–30 64
John 5:22, 24 97
John 5:25 24
John 5:25–28 65
John 5:36 120
John 6:31–58 64
John 6:31–66 118
John 6:35 11
John 6:52 25
John 6:53–56 122
John 6:64 63
John 7:1–27 27
John 7:6 63
John 7:13 80
John 7:14–17 63
John 7:20–30 101

John 7:23 101
John 7:27 100
John 7:30 25, 47
John 7:37–38 122
John 7:38 118, 121
John 7:39 122
John 7—8 82
John 8:12 65
John 8:13–30, 39–58 101
John 8:20 25, 47
John 8:23 98
John 8:24 65
John 8:28 26, 66
John 8:44 98
John 8:46 82
John 8:53, 57 100
John 8:58 66
John 8:59 27
John 9:22 80, 81
John 9:39 98
John 10:7–18 27, 65
John 10:24–25 61, 78, 82
John 10:31 27
John 10:33 100
John 10:36 78
John 11:8, 33, 45, 54 81
John 11:16 101
John 11:25 65
John 11:41–42 63
John 11:45–53 79
John 11:45–54 79
John 11:46–53 80
John 11:47 36
John 11:47–53 68
John 11:50 25
John 11:53 27
John 12:3 61
John 12:27 25
John 12:27–28 47, 50
John 12:28 25
John 12:28b 48
John 12:32 26
John 13:1 25, 47
John 13:1, 3 63, 118
John 13:23 119
John 13:27 63
John 13:30 62
John 13:38 101
John 14:6 65
John 14:16–17, 25–26 120
John 14:28–30 64
John 14—17 61
John 15:26 120
John 16:5, 16 64
John 16:13 120
John 16:31 101

John 16:32 47
John 17:1 25
John 17:1–6 26
John 17:1, 26 98
John 17:4 120
John 18:1 63
John 18:1–11 62
John 18:3 80, 81
John 18:4 118
John 18:5, 6, 8 47, 66
John 18:8–9 66
John 18:10 58, 61
John 18:11 47, 66
John 18:12 81
John 18:12–14, 19–24 80
John 18:12–27 79
John 18:19 81
John 18:19–24 68
John 18:20 82
John 18:23 82
John 18:28 98
John 18:28—19:24 96
John 18:30 100
John 18:31 33, 100
John 18:33 98
John 18:33–39 99
John 18:38 61, 98
John 18:39 100
John 19:2 98
John 19:3 24
John 19:4 98
John 19:4, 6 61
John 19:9 98
John 19:11 100
John 19:13 98, 99
John 19:14 120
John 19:15 100
John 19:17 117
John 19:19–22 100
John 19:21 24
John 19:26 119
John 19:28 118
John 19:29 121
John 19:36 120
John 20:5 61
John 20:8 119
John 20:9–10 61
John 20:15 66
John 20:17 61
John 20:19 80
John 20:19, 20, 27 61
John 20:22 120
John 21 60
John 21:1–19 4
John 21:20–24 119

Acts 2:33 26
Acts 2:34 99
Acts 2:46 78

Acts 2:46 107
Acts 3:1–11 78
Acts 3:13 94
Acts 4:5 77
Acts 4:12 115
Acts 4:27 94
Acts 4—6 36
Acts 5:12, 20–21 78
Acts 5:21 77
Acts 5:31 26, 115
Acts 6:9 102
Acts 7:25 115
Acts 7:56 79
Acts 7:60 55
Acts 9:40 55
Acts 11:26 22
Acts 12 95
Acts 12:12 59
Acts 12:13 75
Acts 13:23 115
Acts 13:28 94
Acts 20:36 55
Acts 21:5 55
Acts 21:14 55
Acts 22:30 77
Acts 22:30—23:9 36
Acts 23:29 95
Acts 25:14 95
Acts 25:25 95
Acts 26:31 95
Acts 28:18 95

Rom. 5:18 126
Rom. 8:34 73

1 Cor. 3:16 70
1 Cor. 7 9
1 Cor. 11 9
1 Cor. 11:23 77
1 Cor. 15:3 51, 124
1 Cor. 15:25 73
1 Cor. 16:22 52

Gal. 4:6 52

Eph. 1:20 73, 99

Phil. 2:6–11 26, 47

Col. 3:1 73

Heb. 1:3 73
Heb. 5:7–8 47, 50
Heb. 8:1 73
Heb. 10:12–13 73
Heb. 12:2 73

Rev. 1:7 52
Rev. 1:17 66
Rev. 21:22 69

INDEX OF AUTHORS AND SUBJECTS

AUTHORS

Ashton 98

Bird 46
Bond 33, 37, 38, 39, 87
Brandon 13
Brown 1, 74, 103, 112, 116, 122
Bultmann 8
Burkitt 9
Burridge 2

Cathcart 70
Crossan 14

Dierx 41
Donnelly 15
Downing 13

Ehrenberg 33
Elliott 46, 69, 84

Fitzmyer 53

Garbrecht 41
Goodman 34, 35, 43
Goulder 60
Green 20

Hill 44
Holleran 46

Jaubert 121
Jeremias 8, 52
Johnson 11
Jones 33
Josephus 15, 28, 29, 30, 33, 34, 35, 36, 39, 41, 42, 43, 68, 71, 80, 81, 107, 118, 125

Lintott 32
Longenecker 88

Matera 77, 83, 93
McGing 37, 38
McLaren 36
Metzger 116

Neill 6
Neirynck 18, 46, 68
Nodet 36

Perrin 10, 73
Philo 37, 38, 39
Porter 1, 11, 14
Puéch 20

Sanders 11, 12, 15, 35, 105
Schürer 43
Schweitzer 6, 7
Senior 85, 89

Shellard 61
Sherwin-White 32, 95

van der Horst 81
Vanhoye 103
Vermes 15, 16, 71

von Wahlde 80

Walaskay 94
Weeden 50
Wrede 6, 8
Wright 6, 11

SUBJECTS

Abba 52, 53
Annas 80, 81, 82, 83, 96
anti-Judaism
  in Matthew 20, 21–2, 88–9, 90–92, 124–5
  in John 124–5
apocalyptic 7, 104–6, 110–12
aqueducts 40, 41, 42
Archelaus 30, 31, 43

beloved disciple 118, 119, 120, 124
blasphemy 73–4

Caiaphas 34, 35, 68, 79, 80, 81
chiasmus 18, 92, 98, 99
chronology of Jesus' mission 5–6, 79–80
criteria for authenticity 9–11
cursus honorum 31, 43
Cynics 13, 14

divorce 3, 9, 70

failure of disciples 19–20, 48–50, 59, 74–5, 76–7
foreknowledge of Jesus 63–4
fulfilment of scripture 21, 51–2, 103, 124

Hanina 15, 16, 71
hellenisation 14, 15
Herod Antipas 28, 95

Herod the Great 12, 13, 30, 34, 35, 43, 44
historicity 2–17, 67–8, 84–6, 86–7, 123–5
Honi 15, 53, 71

Jamnia, Synod of 81
Jesus as
  King 88–9, 99–100, 117–18
  Saviour 115–17
  son of God 20, 73, 76, 78–9, 107–9, 126
  Suffering Servant 74, 124
  Wisdom 82
Jesus Seminar 10, 11
Johannine sarcasm 100–1
John and
  ambiguity 24, 25–6, 65, 80, 97, 99–100, 120
  Christology 64–6
  dualism 98
  judgement 97–8, 99–100
  knowledge of Jerusalem 6, 62–3
  Luke 60–61
  the Church 118–22
  the Hour of Jesus 24–5, 47, 119–20
  the Jews 80–1, 99–100

Last Supper 23, 57, 58, 61, 63, 98, 118, 119, 121
Lukan style 95–6, 116
Luke and
  healing 61–2, 116

John 60–61
prayer 55
the Jews 113–14
Luke as creative historian 116
Luke's great journey 23

Mark and persecution 18–19
Markan
grouping of incidents 79–80
irony 17, 74, 104
sandwiches 18, 68
style 46, 68–9, 84–5, 86
triples 19, 46, 102
Matthean
Beatitudes 20–21
Matthew and
scribes 71
the Jews 87–8

messianic secret 73
midrash 87

Pilate 12, 20, 24, 29, 30, 32, 35, 37–45,
46, 61, 68, 72, 77, 79, 83, 84–101,
104, 115, 118, 123, 124, 125

Roman provincial government 30–45

sanhedrin 19, 21, 35, 36, 37, 68, 77,
79, 83

Temple, destruction and renewal
69–71, 106–7, 114–15

universalism 107

Zealots 13